O God, Tender and Just

Edited by Elizabeth C. Nordbeck

O GOD
TENDER AND JUST

REFLECTIONS and RESPONSES after SEPTEMBER 11, 2001

UNITED CHURCH OF CHRIST

UNITED
CHURCH
PRESS

United Church Press, Cleveland, Ohio 44115
www.ucpress.com
© 2002 by United Church Press

ISBN 0-8298-1534-1

CONTENTS

FOREWORD

BOTH THE MISSION PLANNING COUNCIL OF THE UNITED CHURCH OF CHRIST
and Florence Coppola, executive of the United Church of Christ's National Disaster
Ministries, envisioned the production of several resources that would help people move
to a time of healing and renewal following the terrorist attacks of September 11, 2001.
These included a commemorative book that would share the many voices—both of
anguish and of thoughtful reflection—that emerged following that day in history, a Study
Guide that is part of the book's text, a Bible Study on the Twenty-third Psalm, and a
liturgy of remembrance.

The first task was to find an editor for the book, and, with thanks, seminary professor and church historian Elizabeth Nordbeck agreed to serve. After reading through
hundreds of responses to the tragic events, Beth chose some of the most thoughtful,
inspiring, and hope-filled pieces, organizing them according to the concerns of the writers themselves. Collectively, these responses suggest the many and complex layers of
political, social, and theological issues related to both the events of September 11 and
our responses to them. They call us all to continue to pray for hope from the rubble—
as well as to continue to seek knowledge and act faithfully.

This text is being offered to congregations of the United Church of Christ as a gift,
thanks to the work of a committee of representatives from the denomination's four
Covenanted Ministries. (Copies are also available from United Church Press for individuals and churches that want to use the book for study and reflection.) Committee members who worked closely with the editor were Jan Aerie, Robert Chase, Florence Coppola,
Noelle Damico, Benjamin Guess, Kathy Method, Rod Mundy, Phyllis Richards, Susan
Sanders, Stephanie Spencer, and Madrid Tramble.

Hope is always before those who bear the name of Christ. It is with hope that this
offering is made—hope that healing and wholeness, as well as peace with justice, might
be known by all of God's creation.

Rodney L. Mundy

*Executive for Ministry Interpretation
and Public Relations*

INTRODUCTION

THIS IS A BOOK THAT IS BOTH FOR AND ABOUT THE CHURCH.

It is *for* the church as a special volume commemorating the one-year anniversary of the awful acts of violence that took place on September 11, 2001, when terrorists deliberately crashed airplanes into the World Trade Center in New York and the Pentagon in Washington, D.C. A third plane, apparently failing in an unknown mission of destruction, crashed in a Pennsylvania field. More than three thousand persons from around the world—some of them members of congregations of the United Church of Christ—were killed.

Grief, anger, confusion, fear: These were the emotions that most Americans felt after September 11. Suddenly, the safest, most secure, nation in the world was no longer safe, and even people of faith had far more questions than answers: Where is a loving God in the midst of such carnage? Why do the terrorists hate Americans so much? What can ordinary people do to help? What should Christians know about the causes of this and other kinds of potential violence? How should we think about the future? In the year since the attacks, healing—and some answers—have come for many, thanks in part to the outpourings of sympathy from around the world, the ritual moments of remembrance shared in hundreds of places of worship, and the unprecedented generosity and heroism of men and women as they ministered to those affected most deeply by the tragedy. For others, there remains a strong need to reflect and remember; there are still unanswered questions and unresolved emotions. It is our hope that this volume, filled with thoughtful reflections from pastors and laypeople, Christians and persons of other faiths, scholars and leaders and teachers, will help continue the process of renewal and healing.

To that end, readers will find a useful Study Guide at the end of the book. The guide includes a section on each chapter, with suggested hymn and prayer resources as well as discussion and journaling questions for theological and personal reflection. The Study Guide may be used to focus specifically on the events of September 11 as people continue trying to understand, accept, and interpret them. Additionally, it may be used to reflect more generally on theological and other issues raised by crisis, tragedy, violence, and suffering.

This is also a book *about* the church and the faithful way it responds to crisis. In the days, weeks, and months after September 11, literally thousands of people logged on to the United Church of Christ's Web site <www.ucc.org>. They posted their own reflections about what had happened or shared the helpful words of others. Prayers, essays, letters of condolence and solidarity, sermons, news briefs, and articles swiftly appeared in a spontaneous sharing of thoughts and information. These postings make up the book's primary content.

The envisioners of this volume saw it initially as a chronological account. They predicted that the tone and content of writings on the Web site would shift subtly as initial shock, anger, and calls for retaliatory actions gave way, over time, to more measured and moderated assessments. But this was not the case. From the day after the tragedy and during the several months following, offerings on the denominational Web site remained strikingly consistent in both tone and content. Although the voices and forms differed, these hundreds of postings consistently shared common themes deeply grounded in the faithful, biblical perspective of their writers: Care for those who hurt. Hope for the future. Seek justice, not vengeance. Be informed and be active. Exercise restraint. And trust in God.

And so, this is a book *by* the church itself—men and women who are seeking to understand and to act responsibly and faithfully in the face of events that are, ultimately, incomprehensible and unspeakable. It is structured not chronologically but according to the concerns expressed by all those who chose to share their reflections. I feel both grateful and privileged to have had the opportunity to read not only the few offerings that appear in this volume, but literally hundreds of other moving reflections that space could not accommodate. My special thanks to Noelle Damico, who prepared the Study Guide, and to the planning team, who worked diligently at the eleventh hour to ensure a timely printing on a tight schedule.

Elizabeth C. Nordbeck
Andover Newton Theological School

THE THINGS THAT WE FEAR HAVE COME UPON US

First Responses to September 11, 2001

❧

Truly the thing that I fear
comes upon me, and what I dread befalls
me. I am not at ease, nor am I quiet.
I have no rest, but trouble comes.

—Job 3:25–26

Alas, alas, the great city. . . .
For in one hour all this wealth
has been laid waste.

—Revelation 18:16–17

❧

WHERE WERE YOU ON THE MORNING OF SEPTEMBER 11, 2001? Editor Evan Golder asked readers this question in the October issue of *United Church News*. Like the attack on Pearl Harbor, or the Challenger disaster, or the assassination of John F. Kennedy, certain events permanently inscribe a "before" and "after" in our personal and collective lives.

For many Americans, the attacks on the World Trade center and the Pentagon changed *everything*, not only the immediate rhythms of life. The morning of September 12 was, in the words of United Church of Christ minister Robin Meyers, like "waking up in a different country." Shock, grief, and confusion mingled with fear; words failed altogether. The attacks caused tragic loss of life, above all; but they also precipitated the loss of a certain naiveté, a uniquely American innocence about the reality of violence and evil in the world.

People responded to the tragedy differently, as these articles, letters, and prayers suggest. Some discovered stirrings of patriotism they had not experienced before, even as they struggled with new feelings of insecurity and anxiety. Others tried to understand how such events could have happened in this, the wealthiest and—always before—safest nation in the world. And many simply prayed for guidance and wisdom, calling on God to offer solace to the hurting and wisdom and restraint to those in whose hands the nation's future lay.

Prayer for Service of Remembrance at
Andover Newton Theological School, Newton Centre, Massachusetts,
September 12, 2001

❀

ELIZABETH C. NORDBECK

WE ARE STRANGERS TO OURSELVES, O God, and to one another, but never to you. You know the longings of our souls, the signs too deep for words. In sleeping and in waking, in quiet and in confusion, in despair and in hope, in silence and in sound, you hear the cries of our hearts. Hear us now, as we pray.

Who are we, Lord, that you are mindful of us?
We are bystanders, the ones left disquieted and helpless.
The things we have feared have come upon us;
    what we have dreaded has happened
And we are filled with confusion.

Who are we, Lord, that you are mindful of us?
We are the wounded and hurting, the ones whose groans pour out like water.
We are crushed in body and in spirit;
    we find no solace among the living,
And we are filled with fear.

Who are we, Lord, that you are mindful of us?
We are the angry, the ones who work in shadows and secrecy.
We will do what needs to be done
    to reshape this world as we know it should be.
And we are filled with hatred.

Who are we, Lord?
In these times of trouble and tragedy there is much we do not know.
But this we know:
Whoever we are, whatever we do, you are mindful of us.
Your everlasting arms will comfort all who come to you,
    And your judgment will fall down upon those who do not follow your ways
    of love and peace.

Help us, we pray, on this bright morning when brightness seems false and
    light fails us utterly.
Help us to live peaceably with the things we know, and the things we cannot know.
Grant us the grace to speak hope in the midst of despair.
Grant us the courage to return love for hatred.

Grant us the wisdom to believe that vengeance is yours, not ours.
And grant us the compassion to minister to those from whom despair and
    hatred are the bitter fuel that keeps soul and body together.

We pray in the deep confidence that this world is yours and all that is in it. And we pray in the name of the One who came to us as the Prince of Peace. Amen.

Elizabeth C. Nordbeck is the Moses Brown Professor of Ecclesiastical History at Andover Newton Theological School, Newton Centre, Massachusetts.

Reflections of the General Minister and President of the United Church of Christ

Tuesday, September 11, 2001

❁

JOHN H. THOMAS

MY FIRST TRIP TO BERLIN, part of an ecumenical visit to church partners in Germany, Switzerland, and Hungary, was already rich with personal and historical association. Berlin is where many of the defining political events of my generation took place—the Berlin airlift, the Wall, the beginning of reunification, and the end of the Cold War. Here is where my father-in-law served the American Church in Berlin during the dramatic years of the 1930s. To stay at a church-run hotel called the "Dietrich Bonhoeffer-Haus" was, itself, to be reminded of a key part of the Christian story in the twentieth century.

Peter Makari, area executive for the Middle East and Europe of the Common Global Ministries Board, and I began the morning of September 11 on a drive with Bill and Sabine Downey, retired associates of the United Church Board for World Ministries who had done pastoral work in Berlin in the 1970s, '80s, and '90s. The Downeys drove us out of the city past the Brandenburg Gate, along a street that once housed many of the Nazi ministries and the famous Templehof Airport, past the former site of the Gestapo headquarters, and by one of the few remaining remnants of the Wall. Our journey took us to Frankfurt on the Oder, a former Hanseatic city on what is now the Polish border, in part of what once was the German Democratic Republic. There we visited Lisa and Steve Smith and their son David, missionaries of the Common Global Ministries Board who are serving a parish of the Evangelical Church in Berlin-Brandenburg, one of the regional churches of the Evangelical Church of the Union, our partner in Kirchengemeinschaft since 1981. Our visit also included a special gathering of church leaders and press to present an Award of Affirmation to Dr. Rolf Wischnath, general superintendent of the Cottbus Region of the Berlin-Brandenburg Church. Wischnath was to have received his award at the General Synod-Assembly in July but had been ill and unable to travel. The award recognized Wischnath's decisive leadership role in opposing the violence perpetrated by right-wing hate groups against asylum-seekers and ethnic minorities. He is president of the Brandenburg Action Alliance against Violence and is well known in church and society for his commitment. The award ceremony was well attended by the press, and Wischnath used this festive occasion to draw public attention to the plight of two Kosovar families being threatened with deportation by the state.

As toasts were exchanged at a closing reception, one of the reporters returned, shaken, to inform us of the unfolding catastrophe in New York and Washington. Dr. Wischnath led our group in prayer and then accompanied us to the television station, where staff made provision for us to watch the coverage of the terrorist attacks and call colleagues in Cleveland. Reporters interviewed me for radio and television coverage, barely able to control their emotions. These members of a profession often caricatured as callous and insensitive sent us on our way back to Berlin with embraces of consolation and care. And Wischnath, whom we had come to honor for his prophetic ministry, became our pastor in a parting blessing. Together with the Smiths and their pastoral colleagues, this was for me a profound moment of partnership.

On our return to Berlin at eight o'clock in the evening, we were met by Friedrich Demke, ecumenical officer of the Evangelical Church of the Union in Berlin, informing us that we were asked to participate in a hastily called ecumenical vigil to be held at the Berliner Dom, the restored Protestant Cathedral, an event that would be hosted by the Bishop of the Evangelical Church of Berlin-Brandenburg, Wolfgang Huber, and the Roman Catholic Archbishop of Berlin, Cardinal Sterzinsky. Several thousand Berliners filled the church and spilled out into the damp, chilly streets. The leaders of the major political parties, the mayor of Berlin, and the federal justice minister joined ordinary Berliners to sing and pray. I was welcomed as a church partner and as a kind of representative of the American people in this remarkable outpouring of grief, tears, and consolation. As the cardinal, bishop, and I moved from the sanctuary to the crowd outside, we were met by hundreds of mostly young people singing songs for peace, a moment made significant and poignant by the fact that one of the songs was in Hebrew and another was our "We Shall Overcome." Countless strangers took my hand and said, "We are so sorry."

Our day ended as it did for many—sitting in front of television news and telephoning friends and family in the New York area to reassure ourselves of their well-being. But for Peter and me, there was much more as we reflected on this incredible day. We had gone to a part of the world that many once feared would be the place World War III might begin, only to watch terrifying destruction in cities close to home. We had come to express the support of the United Church of Christ and the Christian Church (Disciples of Christ) to our partner church as it struggles with the largely atheistic, post-socialist context of the former East Germany, but instead we received the care of that church in the face of our own national tragedy. We came to honor the struggle against violence by courageous colleagues far from home, only to watch violence come home to us in painful, frightening, and intimate ways, and we learned that overcoming violence must be our own struggle as well. We woke up to a city heavy with ominous historical meaning; we went to bed embraced by Berliners gentle in their care and extravagant in their compassion. For all its horror, as yet not fully grasped, it was a graced day.

At the ecumenical service I offered this prayer. May it be ours in the coming days:

> Loving and eternal God, who promises to wipe away tears in a time without mourning or pain, you bring comfort and consolation to those who trust in you. Tonight we give thanks for this sign of companionship and consolation by the people of Berlin for the people of my native land. We give thanks for

this moment, when the church is able to see beyond its own separation to the gift of its unity in Christ. Hear us now as we pray for those whose loved ones have died today, for those who struggle with pain and injury, for those who even now risk their lives to rescue others. Guide the leaders of the United States and their colleagues around the world, that they may turn away from violence and vengeance, seeking the way that leads to reconciliation, justice, and hope. This we pray.

And the congregation responded in the ancient song, "Kyrie eleison, Kyrie eleison, Kyrie eleison." Mercy. Let us be so.

From the United Church of Christ Web site <www.ucc.org>, September 11, 2001. Reprinted by permission.

"With Liberty and Justice for All"

The America We Must Defend

❀

CHARLES HAYNES

THE DAY AFTER.

From my office in Arlington, Va., I see smoke still pouring out of the Pentagon. Rescuers continue to risk their lives as hope fades for finding more survivors.

Day and night, desperate friends and relatives of victims stand near the wreckage here and in New York, praying for a miracle.

Millions of us join their vigil in our hearts. We offer prayers, fly flags, donate blood, send money, but we still feel helpless in the face of unspeakable tragedy. Words fail us.

America is forever changed.

It will be many weeks before we fully grasp the magnitude and implications of these horrific events. But we already know that life in our nation will never be the same.

Never again can we take our safety and freedom for granted. Terrorism is no longer a crisis that mostly affects people in other lands. Terrorism is now a fact of life in the United States, aimed at shaking the foundations of our republic.

What kind of nation will we be?

Much depends on how we respond to this supreme test of our national character. We can react in ways that restrict our liberties and divide our nation, or we can respond in ways consistent with the ideals and principles that define America.

Many of the early signs are heartening.

Who among us will ever forget the thousands of police, firefighters, and medical personnel in Arlington and New York who rushed in to help—and in many cases sacrificed their lives? Or the images of countless volunteers or long lines of people waiting for hours to give blood?

Consider also the resolve and unity of our national leaders. With one voice, they resolve to defend freedom, but to do so in concert with our allies around the world and in ways that uphold our commitment to justice.

We are a caring people. We are a determined nation. This bodes well for the nation we will become in the aftermath of this tragedy.

Sadly, however, there are some Americans—let's hope it's a small minority—who are responding with hate and fear. Less than twenty hours after the first attack, I had already received e-mail messages condemning Islam and threatening violence. One writer called for the deportation of all Muslims "back to the desert hell holes where they come from."

As I write this, news reports are coming in about death threats and violence directed at American Muslims. Bullets shatter the windows of a Texas mosque. Bricks hit an Islamic bookstore in northern Virginia. Vandals deface Islamic centers in various parts of the country. Muslim leaders advise American Muslims who wear Islamic attire to stay out of public areas for the immediate future.

This is the dark side of America—the America of militia movements, hate groups, white supremacists, anti-immigration zealots, race-mongers, and religious extremists. These are the people who attack freedom in the name of freedom, much like the hijackers themselves.

Their numbers may be small. But if we aren't careful, if we don't speak out, the voices of hatred can infect the body politic in this crisis time.

That's why we need to be very clear that authentic Muslims could have had nothing to do with the attacks on the Pentagon and the World Trade Center. Those who carried out these murderous acts are evil criminals without conscience.

Whatever religion they invoke in support of their "cause," they do not, by definition, have anything to do with the genuine teachings of Islam, Judaism, Christianity, or any other of the world's major faiths. These terrorists are no more "Islamic" than the killers in Northern Ireland are "Catholic" or "Protestant."

Unfortunately, promoters of hate and fear ignore such distinctions. They exploit times like this by creating scapegoats and perpetuating false stereotypes. If we care about our nation, we must not let that happen.

The America we must defend in the coming weeks and months is the America of freedom and justice for Muslim Americans, Christian Americans, Jewish Americans, or Americans of any other religion or creed. Defending the rights of all citizens is at the heart of what it means to be an American.

In the near term, we must find and punish the perpetrators of the attacks on our nation. And we must take all the necessary steps to prevent future attacks.

But in the long term, the best and surest defense of freedom is the practice of freedom.

As I write these words, I look up to see that the smoke has finally cleared at the Pentagon, exposing the gaping hole in the side of our nation's symbol of military might.

But then I look across the river and see the Lincoln Memorial gleaming in the afternoon sun. And I recall the words inscribed there, spoken during another great test of the American character and the American nation:

> We here highly resolve that these dead shall not have died in vain—that this nation, under God, shall have a new birth of freedom—and that government of the people, by the people, for the people, shall not perish from the earth.

Charles Haynes is senior scholar at the First Amendment Center where he specializes in religion issues related to the Constitution. His e-mail address is <chaynes@freedomforum.org>.

Reflections

September 16, 2001

❀

JIM BUNDY

Scriptures: Psalm 122 and 121; 2 Corinthians 4:7–10; Ephesians 3:14–17; Zechariah 4:1–6; Matthew 5:3–10; Micah 6:6–8

LIKE MANY OF YOU, I'm sure, I am in no way through processing what has happened, and my feelings shift from grief over the loss of life and the pain so many people will live with, to worry about what the future holds, to thinking about what I or we ought to say or think or feel or do. I have found it hard to say very much at all, even to myself, while people are still trying to save lives and recover bodies and while just grief for individuals and for this world seems like the most appropriate response . . .

First of all, I am concerned and prayerful that the direction of our response not be to retreat into a kind of militant tribalism. When Christians say "our people," when I as a Christian say "my people," I do not mean simply other Christians. If my identity is that I am a child of God, then my people are God's people, and God's people know no boundaries of religion or nation.

It is not so much a time to rally as Americans but to rally as human beings, affirming in whatever ways it may be possible to do so our oneness as human beings and asking God's blessing, not only on America but on all nations and peoples. This will include standing with those Muslims in our country, some of whom have already been scapegoated. It will include remembering that terrorism, torture, genocide, and other forms of sickening violence know no national boundaries. It will include struggling somehow to find ways not to affirm our Americanness but to affirm our humanity in the days ahead.

And, finally, I am concerned and prayerful that our actions, to use Paul's words, be rooted and grounded in love . . . what else is there for us to do, but to continue now the tasks that were ours a week ago and that remain now ever more important—to seek justice, to love mercy, to walk humbly with God, and to be rooted and grounded in love. May our hearts be set on such things as these. Amen.

Reflections for Sojourners United Church of Christ, Charlottesville, Virginia. September 2001. Used by permission.

Waking Up in a Different Country

❀

ROBIN R. MEYERS

MOST OF THE TIME, I like being a preacher. In fact, the only time I can remember dreading to speak and wondering what on earth to say was on April 23, 1995, the first Sunday after the bombing of the Murrah Federal building. I thought that was hard. I think this is impossible.

Early on Wednesday morning, after a long and restless night, I opened my eyes and, just for a moment, as humans sometimes do, I thought that maybe, just maybe, it had all been a dream. A terrible, horrible nightmare—but only a dream from which we would all awaken and, in great relief, go on with our lives.

For just a moment, I thought perhaps the Twin Towers of the World Trade Center were still standing; that maybe, just maybe, it was just one more Hollywood fiction, and someone had just pulled off the world's most incredible special effect. Just for a moment, I thought maybe all the planes in the country were still flying, all the baseball and football games are still being played, all the passengers who climbed aboard the day before had gotten where they were going and were waking up in their beds and stirring about for their morning coffee.

For just a moment, I thought that maybe the Pentagon had *not* been sliced in half, and the president had *not* been afraid to return to Washington, and thousands of people did *not* lie crushed to death beneath the rubble of what had once been a colossal concrete village for 50,000 of God's diverse people.

Just for a moment, I thought that perhaps there were *no* rescue workers pawing at that wretched pile like ants filling up their buckets with pieces of people's lives, and pieces of people, and that they would *not* have to find their own brothers and sisters in there, the firemen and policemen who went in, brought people out, went back in, brought people out, went back in, and then never came out.

Just for a moment, I thought that perhaps I had awakened in the very same country in which I awakened the morning before, but it was my thinking that was wishful; it was my denial that was dream-like. Now have the country we love and the world we know been changed forever.

On Tuesday morning, which broke so fair and bright, I was doing my very favorite thing in the world—taking Cass to school. I like it not only because we have a few moments together but because, even at the age of eight, Cass still holds my hand when we walk across the street and into the school, and then he turns it loose lest any classmate should see him being "uncool." But the feel of his hand in my hand, which will not last very much longer, is one of the sweetest things I know.

We listen to NPR on the way; the whole Meyers clan are confirmed NPR junkies (we don't think the day has started properly if we haven't listened to *Stardate*), and at about five minutes till eight o'clock, in the middle of the news broadcast, I heard Bob Edwards (he of the mellifluous voice) say, "We have a report of a plane having hit one of the World Trade Towers, and the details are sketchy. It is believed to be a small, twin-engine plane."

Would that it had been. I made my way to the coffee shop and called Shawn. She said "A second plane has hit the other tower," and, in a voice I know from all the years is not given to exaggeration, she said, "It's bad . . . very bad."

I headed on to the university, where the dean of the college and other faculty members were gathered around a television set in that strange, dreadful silence that marks our worst moments. There we watched in utter disbelief as each of the towers collapsed. I don't know about you, but I never even considered that the buildings might fall down. That the upper floors would burn and many people would perish, yes—but not that the whole thing would come crashing down.

And because we live in an electronic village, we watched it all in real time and knew that each collapse meant witnessing the death of thousands of people. It was too much, and many of us began to want to turn away, but we couldn't. How many times have we seen the planes hit the buildings? How many times have we seen people running from the cloud of dust and ashes? How many times have we seen, and will we see, human beings falling out of the sky?

Even though we are a people hardened by violent images, it was all too much; it became literally "unbearable." The disbelief turned to shock, and now the shock has turned to a smoldering and even indiscriminate anger. We have found ourselves clinging to our children and to one another. And let's be honest now—for the pulpit demands nothing less—we have begun to fear even more what may happen next.

The nation is united by the most volatile of all emotions: by grief, by anger, and by an overwhelming sense that something decisive must be done to punish the evil that we witnessed. We have even brought out of retirement the world's deadliest word: war. To say it, just to speak it aloud in the temples of power, is to create the most frightening of all human realities and to prepare citizens for any eventuality.

But if we are indeed at war—and that decision has already been made for us— then it is a war the likes of which we have never waged before. In all the comparisons to Pearl Harbor, said Daniel Shor, we forget that on that December morning, the enemy left its return address. We knew who did it, and we knew what we had to do.

These are the modern day kamikazes, and yet they are not acting overtly on behalf of a nation but on behalf of a cause that gathers up all the hatred of the West and mixes it with a demonic belief in a vengeful God—a God who they believe condones the shedding of innocent blood and even rewards their martyrdom with eternal bliss.

This means that we are going to war not against a nation but against the newest and most deadly form of hatred. Since it is an entirely different kind of war and an entirely different kind of enemy, we will have to wage it in an entirely different way— and yet there are no manuals for this. That we are looking for a needle in a haystack is so frustrating that there have already been calls, in the words of George Will, to "burn down the whole haystack."

I cannot imagine that there has ever been a time in American history when it was more important for us to recognize the difference, the profound difference, between justice and vengeance. If we do not, we run the risk of granting the terrorists an even greater victory than the one they think they have already won. For what they crave more than death itself is to paralyze us with fear and to warp our moral sensibilities in a way that more nearly matches their own.

This is exactly why the church, together with people of faith everywhere, must do what we have always been called on to do: speak truth to power. For if we do not have anything *different* to say to those who often call on us to bless whatever it is they have already decided to do, then we are but mere accessories.

In other words, what words must come from the pulpit? What changes, I want to know, when a man or woman stands in a pulpit—as opposed to standing behind a Pentagon briefing lecture, or a State Department podium, or even behind the desk in the Oval Office? How does the institution of the church speak differently to the world at a time like this?

First of all, we should resist the impulse to co-opt the tragedy for any personal agendas. I am a politically opinionated person myself but not right now. It does not help anyone to hear an Oklahoma congressman tell us that what this proves is that we need a missile defense or that Clinton failed to spend enough money for intelligence during his eight years in office. Nor does it help anyone to hear Jerry Falwell tell us that the attack is God's way of giving us "what we deserve" for our wickedness, for our abortions, for our tolerance of pagans, and for "throwing God out of the public square."

Because anyone who doesn't think we are a deeply religious people obviously didn't listen to that magnificent service from the National Cathedral on Friday. Though he was halting and stooped over, I have never heard Billy Graham so eloquent. I have never heard such desperately beautiful music or seen so many powerful people so obviously shaken to the core and so unapologetically in need of the comfort and wisdom of God.

So the first thing that religious people do is not to look for someone to blame but to give everyone a chance to *grieve* and to admit that our hearts are broken—all of our hearts are broken. Every single life lost last Tuesday was precious and sacred, and the connection we feel to those who lost loved ones (a connection we can feel with a dreadful kind of clarity in this city) runs deeper than words. People all over the world have been singing our national anthem. A European woman, speaking at a rally, said it best: "In these times, we are all New Yorkers; we are all Americans."

That's what we do first, if we are religious people. We console. We push aside all the barriers that normally keep us separated from one another and we say, "You can pray here; you can worship here; you can cry here," because our first and last responsibility is to love.

The second thing people of faith can do is to offer a clear and unapologetic word of *restraint* as our nation discerns what its response will be. People of faith share the same anger, the same overwhelming sense that "something must be done." We, too, demand that those responsible for this horror be found and brought to justice.

But we must say something else, something that will be hard to say and even harder for people to hear. And that is pray for an unearthly *patience* in deciding how to retaliate lest countless more innocent people die. We must pray for the president and members of Congress to seek not just the wisdom of Machiavelli but also the wisdom of God.

The third thing that people of faith can do is face without flinching the deep and profound questions about what this will do to us as a nation. In the words of Jim Wallis, who preached in this pulpit not long ago and heads the *Sojourners* community in Washington, D.C., "The terrorists have offered us a stark view of the world they would create, where the remedy to every human grievance and injustice is a resort to the random and cowardly violence of revenge—even against the most innocent." He continues:

> Having taken thousands of our lives, attacked our national symbols, forced our political leaders to flee their chambers of governance, disrupted our work and families, and struck fear into the hearts of our children, the terrorists must feel victorious.
>
> But we can deny them their victory by refusing to submit to a world created in their image. Terrorism inflicts not only death and destruction but also emotional oppression to further its aims. We must not allow this terror to drive us away from being the people God has called us to be. We assert the vision of community, tolerance, compassion, justice, and the sacredness of human life, which lies at the heart of all our religious traditions. America must be a safe place for all our citizens in all their diversity. It is especially important that our citizens who share national origins, ethnicity, or religion with whoever attacked us are, themselves, protected among us.
>
> Our American illusion of invulnerability has been shattered. From now on, we will look at the world in a different way, and this attack on our life as a nation will become a test of our national character. Let us make the right choices in this crisis—to pray, act, and unite against the bitter fruits of division, hatred, and violence. Let us rededicate ourselves to global peace, human dignity, and the eradication of the injustice that breeds rage and vengeance.
>
> As we gather in our houses of worship, let us begin a process of seeking the healing and grace of God.

Those of us in Oklahoma City know, because we are in a unique position to know, that what appears to be a completely random act, dismissed as incomprehensible because the evil it represents is so incomprehensible, has its roots in the real world and in the hatred and desperation that breeds terrorism. We need to work for a world that breeds fewer terrorists and then work for a world that one day produces none. To do this, we will have to ask ourselves painful and soul-searching questions. But that's what people of faith can do—because we have the resources of God at our disposal.

Because we are people of faith, we will not just try to understand what happened but why it happened. As in the Oklahoma City bombing, so much attention was focused on recovery that very little was ever focused on cause. And, especially, to my way of thinking, focused on the nation-wide network of hate-mongers who rule the world of AM radio in all its childish machismo and who deal in fear and loathing and paranoia as if they were life's only real currency. Because we raised up our own terrorist, and, yet, we do not consider ourselves to be a nation that "harbors terrorists," do we? The enemy here is hatred itself.

Because we are people of faith, we do not go out and buy guns and ammunition or create panic at gas stations. Nor do we think for one minute that we have a corner on the market for heroism in Oklahoma, because we know that countless acts of heroism occurred in New York City and in Washington, D.C. And even aboard the plane that never made it to its intended target—which was probably the White House or the Capitol Building—passengers who knew they were going to die did something to keep other people from dying.

In what is often described as the gruffest and most unfeeling of American cities, there were remarkable displays of human compassion. Not only from those who could not be kept out of the buildings in their rescue efforts and perished in the line of duty, but from ordinary people who carried those who could not walk down stairwells and through the streets and across the Brooklyn Bridge in a bizarre but remarkably ordered mass exodus from what had become a war zone.

We have grown up poking fun at New Yorkers, and preachers have made sermonic hay out of their depravities—and there was panic to be sure—but there was no looting, no anarchy, and no sudden loss of the best human instincts. People helped other people. People wept for other people. Grown men do indeed cry. Strong nations do indeed weep. The truth is, and we feel it, that we have all lost thousands of our relatives.

In the days to come, we will have to turn this numbness into a solemn determination, this outpouring of patriotism into a unity of purpose, not just a unity of rage. What God will ask of us now is more than we could possibly manage on our own, and if we think that we are entirely on our own, to balance the scales of the universe as if we were God, then we really *will* be on our own, and God will be as unable to help us as God was unable to stop what took place on that dark Tuesday.

There is hope, of course—because that's the commodity that we trade in, even when the stock market is shut down. But we don't just buy and sell it. We *live by it*. And there is, in the end, no acceptable alternative to hope.

But that's not all. We live by the wisdom of the ages, because it has brought us this far. And most of all, we live by the unfathomable love of God—made personal to us by one who died to break the cycle of violence. We call on that love now—as urgently and as fretfully as a child, separated from its mother, calls out to find her.

Dear God, do not leave us to wander alone, fashioning our own fantasies of revenge, but call us instead to *follow*. Teach us, in this inconsolable moment, of an incomprehensible love that will have the last word. For now we are all in this together— fighting the evil of hatred—*wherever it exists.*

For if last Tuesday seemed like a nightmare to us, consider for a moment what a terrorist would think to be *his* worst nightmare. You know it, of course you do.

It's love . . .

The Love that will not let us go . . .

God Bless America.

PASTORAL PRAYER FOR SUNDAY, SEPTEMBER 16, 2001

Lord of Life, we come before you and we say together with one broken heart: Help us to live these days in the light of your wisdom, your patience, and your understanding of justice. Do not leave us alone, for we have never needed you more; do not let us forget what greatness is and what greatness requires; do not let us forget all the goodness that still exists in the world and the hope we share for a different future. Bind up the wounds that run deep, and fill the aching void we feel with a determination to make the world safer for everyone. Be with those who lost loved ones and comfort them as only you can. Help us to lock arms with one another and then to put them around everyone and everything we can. We have all lost members of our family; we have all lost an irreplaceable measure of innocence; we have all been choking on the dust of this horrible week. The time has come to measure our faith and to depend on it more than ever. You have not abandoned us, and we will not abandon you. Come to us, abide with us—in this land we love whose heart is broken . . . in Christ's name we pray. Amen.

Sermon delivered by Robin Meyers at Mayflower Congregational Church, Oklahoma City, Oklahoma, September 16, 2001. Copyright © 2001 Robin Meyers. Reprinted by permission.

Religion News Service Commentary on Patriotism

❀

Tom Ehrich

LIKE MANY WHOSE LIVES WERE DISRUPTED by the Vietnam War, I became confused about patriotism.

As a child, I had clarity. Patriotism meant stirring songs, the Pledge of Allegiance, the flag in our classroom, photos of my father in uniform, collecting candidates' lapel pins, feeling grief when President Kennedy was assassinated.

But then patriotism got confused with politics. As an unpopular war proceeded, some claimed that true "patriots" were those who held one set of views, and all others betrayed flag and country.

Maybe it is always thus. Maybe partisans always seize the powerful symbols of patriotism to advance their cause. They do so with religion and race, as well, sometimes joining all three in a powerful demagogic brew.

I lost more than innocence. I lost touch with pledge and the anthem. If patriotism meant one angry slice of the American pie and not the foundation on which we all walked, if the symbols of patriotism could became weapons in a fight against each other, familiar rituals lost their joy.

Terrorists attacking our nation's largest city and capitol have cleared that air.

This is our homeland under attack. Not the Republican Party or the Democratic Party, not liberals or conservatives, not hateful suspicions, not economic theories, not a majority race or a majority religion, not one set of "family values" versus another, but our homeland, this "sweet land of liberty."

On the first Sunday of this new era, leading worship in the next county, we set aside the usual hymns and liturgical niceties. We substituted patriotic songs. I asked a veteran (U.S. Marines, Lebanon, 1957) to carry the American flag in procession.

I could hardly sing a word of "America," not because I was still confused about patriotism, but because years of loss surged to the surface, and I needed to compose myself.

Instead of ritual words, I told about my week since the attacks began. I asked the faithful to tell where they were on Tuesday and how their week had gone. They told powerful stories of worry, pain, anger, disbelief, shutting down, clinging to family.

I offered brief homiletic guidance, as well, but mainly I was confirmed in my belief that this is a time for us to talk, not to orate; to listen to each other, not to stake out positions.

Driving home, I listened to the start of a BBC concert. An American conductor happened to be at the podium in London. He said the British musicians had altered the program and would perform "from our hearts and souls to yours."

From the nation whose shelling inspired the original came: "O say can you see, by the dawn's early light, what so proudly we hailed at the twilight's last gleaming?"

I sang along, as best I could manage.

As if for the first time, the anthem was not the backdrop to American athletes preening at the Olympics, not a prelude to some political convention that would marginalize all but true believers, not the comforting ritual whose "Amen" is "Play ball!"

Composed nearly two hundred years ago, the last time America was attacked by a regressive society that found American freedom threatening, the anthem suddenly gave voice to a live question.

Through rockets and bombs, through the smoke of "war's desolation," is the flag still there? Is "the land of the free" intact?

We must not let patriotism get squandered again. We will disagree in these tense times. Some will cry for vengeance, others for restraint. Some will pick up arms eagerly, some reluctantly, some not at all. Some will rally around the president, and others will question his every move. Some will demand justice through missiles, and others will insist that we study hatred toward America.

Patriotism isn't the property of one political persuasion. It is the ground on which we all speak freely, disagree openly, hold our leaders accountable, and worship as we feel called.

The "star-spangled banner" waves over a land where mosque, synagogue, and church can share an intersection, where flaws can be mended, where "liberty in law" is real, and where brotherhood—multihued, multivalued, sometimes offensive, never complete, but always yearned for—does spread "from sea to shining sea."

Tom Ehrich is a writer and computer consultant managing large-scale database implementations. An Episcopal priest, he lives in Durham, North Carolina.

Peering into the "Dark Abyss"

View from an Overlook

❀

J. MARTIN BAILEY

CLOSE TO OUR HOME is a craggy overlook where we frequently take guests for spectacular views of New York City. On a clear night, you look north and see the diamond necklace of the George Washington Bridge; to the south, you pick out the sparkle of the Statue of Liberty. You watch planes circle to land at LaGuardia, Kennedy, or Newark airports.

We went there the night of the great blackout and peered into a dark abyss. Over the years, we watched the World Trade Center being built, and we witnessed the first night the windows were all lighted. On some misty days, we could see the twin towers rise mysteriously above the clouds.

On September 11, there was only gray smoke. An awesome pillar of smoke.

Then, the television images, crowds gathered at churches, the president's speech, and the flags—all these prompt memories. As President Bush rallied the nation, I heard echoes from my boyhood when we huddled around a big brown Zenith radio to hear President Roosevelt describe a day of infamy. I also recalled the gravelly voice of President Johnson, not long after John F. Kennedy was killed, insist on civil rights legislation, startling his largely white audience with a litany of, "We shall overcome."

The uncertainty that followed the events of September 11 brought other memories as well. On the eve of the Gulf War, I was part of a delegation that went to Baghdad, hoping to carry a word of reason to Saddam Hussein. He wouldn't see us. But we saw his arrogant parade grounds and a lurid exhibit of modern art dominated, strangely, by a huge oil painting of Jesus weeping over Jerusalem. A few weeks later, Desert Storm demonstrated both American military might and the fact that warfare sometimes complicates the struggle for justice and peace.

Nor can I forget the ugly explosions we heard from our recent office near the YMCA in East Jerusalem. That day, suicide bombers left innocent lives and hopes for peace mortally wounded. There also was the night when Yitsak Rabin was gunned down. Frightening times. Sad memories.

Two threads hold this contemporary tapestry of agony and fear together.

One thread is the comforting ministry of the church. When we learned about the attack on Pearl Harbor, all my family could think about was my uncle, a civilian construction engineer on Wake Island. My grandmother found great comfort from the church and finally was able to rejoice when she learned that my uncle was alive as a prisoner of war.

The other thread is the prophetic witness of the church. That small Iowa town in the early '40s was an unlikely place for the voice of reason. But word trickled in that

American citizens of Japanese ancestry had been herded into detention camps on the West Coast, and members of a tiny church spoke out. Their convictions made a lasting impression on at least one teenager.

Today, the churches surround with compassion and love those whose lives have suddenly been turned upside down. Prayers in our New Jersey churches these days are poignantly personal: For a neighbor, whose office was on the 102nd floor. For the family of a friend who made a final telephone call. For one member, planning his retirement, who had breakfast with his broker at Windows on the World. For a young woman, who still works long hours as a police officer. For another woman, who is seeking new homes for pets that suddenly need adoption. And for worried friends in the Middle East—Jews, Christians, and Muslims—who yearn for peace rather than continued turmoil and destruction.

In a state where anger, like grief, is close to the emotional surface, the churches are working with mosques and synagogues to preserve human dignity, to counsel against racial and ethnic profiling, and to discourage the wanton destruction that demands an eye for an eye.

Soon we will return to our craggy overlook. For us it has become a viewpoint as well.

Rev. J. Martin Bailey is the former editor of both the United Church Herald *and* A.D. Magazine.

From *United Church News* (October 2001): A4. Reprinted by permission.

Where Were You on the Morning of September 11?

❀

W. Evan Golder

I WAS ON THE PHONE, talking with my grandson, when he told me the news. I didn't believe him. He must have turned on the television, seen a disaster movie, and assumed it was real, I thought. When my son confirmed the tragedy, I clicked the remote to see for myself. Then I grabbed my keys and drove to where my wife, Deborah, was walking in the park. I hugged her and tried to tell her what had happened, but I was too choked up. No words came.

Some events make such a difference in our personal histories that we remember them not only for themselves but also for where we were at the time and what we were doing. Consider, for example, the killings of John F. Kennedy or Martin Luther King Jr. or the bombing of Pearl Harbor.

These days changed our lives. They ended our innocence ("assassinations don't happen here" or "the oceans will protect us" or "this happens only in the movies"), or they refocused our values.

During these events, we could have been any number of places, but, because of their enormity, the times and places are forever etched in our histories. This reminds us of how we responded. Did we stop what we were doing? Or keep right on? Did we try to contact a loved one? Or want to be alone? Did we try to learn more? Or try to escape the onslaught of media reports? In thinking about this, we learn a bit more about ourselves.

This terrorist attack put life in perspective, at least for a while. What once seemed important—Will my clothes be back from the cleaners in time? Will my favorite team make the playoffs?—didn't seem to matter all that much in the horror of all those lives lost. As the plane sliced through the World Trade Tower, over and over and over again, all week long in the video replays, it sliced the trivial from many lives. I heard people talk of changing their lifestyles to using kinder words, taking more significant actions, living out more sensitive attitudes.

Such changes are how we begin to act out the biblical instruction, "Conduct yourselves wisely toward outsiders, making the most of time" (Col. 4:5). Most of our time is uneventful; in T.S. Eliot's words, we measure out our lives with coffee spoons. But a morning as calamitous as that of September 11 is a moment in time unlike any other. In the midst of our horror and our shock, our sadness and our grieving, our rage and our anger, comes a God-given opportunity. This time is ripe—but what will we do when we pick this fruit?

Does it matter where you or I were on that troubled morning of September 11? That morning now has meaning far beyond other mornings. At the moment, we can see only dimly through the fallen ash of pulverized buildings, bodies, and planes. We do have St. Paul's assurance (Rom. 8:38–39) that neither death, nor life, nor angels, nor rulers, nor hijackers, nor terrorists . . . will be able to separate us from the love of God in Christ Jesus our Lord.

We also have W. H. Auden's reminder, "In the meantime, there [is] . . . the Time Being to redeem from insignificance." For that, we need God's help.

Rev. W. Evan Golder is editor of the national edition of United Church News.

Reprinted from *United Church News*, on-line ed. <www.ucc.org/ucnews/oct01/current.htm>, October 2001. Used by permission.

To the Congregations of the Christian Church
(Disciples of Christ) and the United Church of Christ

September 12, 2001

✦

STEPHANIE SPENCER

DEAR FRIENDS IN CHRIST,

The destruction and carnage of the airplane crashes into the World Trade Center towers, the Pentagon, and the Pennsylvania countryside have burned images into our minds of the worst that people's anger and violence can do. We are weakened with horror at seeing people falling from the Trade Center towers, of people cowering in the dust storms that followed the towers' collapse, of people standing in terrible awe of the Pentagon's burning and collapsing. We have never seen these images broadcast from America. It is outrageous and infuriating that our country can be attacked like this. It is the most unlawful and unjust act to kill thousands of people because someone is angry with our government.

Some people are saying that the terrorist who planned this attack lives in Afghanistan and that he is hiding and training his followers there, supported by the government. President Bush said to the world on Tuesday night that, "We will make no distinction between the terrorists who committed these acts and those who harbor them." Who harbors this man? Who is the Afghan government?

Who harbors this terrorist? I traveled to Afghanistan in May of this year, and I have more images of unimaginable destruction and suffering burned into my mind. In Afghanistan, there has been twenty-two years of uninterrupted war. In Afghanistan, there has been four years of uninterrupted drought. In addition to having no rain, orchards and fields have been destroyed by bombing. In every city, hundreds of thousands of people have come from the villages looking for food and shelter from war. The government cannot provide for these people's needs.

Who is the Afghan government? In Afghanistan, the government is run by a group of the most fundamentalist religious leaders in the Muslim world. This government enforces a dress code for men and women with arrests, beatings on the street, and stonings. This government has closed all schools and colleges and does not allow anyone to be taught to read. This government does not allow women to work, to leave their houses, or to attend schools. This government was not elected or chosen by the people.

I have images in my mind of roads have not been repaired or repaved for at least ten years, of houses in the capital, Kabul, with no electrical service available. On every street, bombed buildings have concrete and steel walls hanging from them. There has not been any cleanup or rebuilding for at least five years.

I have images of refugee camps where people are living in mud-brick houses and in tents, where there is not one tree or bush or patch of grass as far as the eye can see. These camps in neighboring Pakistan hold hundreds of thousands of people. Some people have lived in these camps for ten years.

I have an image of a woman cooking lunch for the office staff on a gas stove placed on the floor, serving plates of food, which all of the women staff ate together sitting on the floor. Even the cook had attended college. Most women were the only members of their extended family earning any wage. The government has now closed this office, and the women now have no jobs, their families have lost the income that supported five or ten people, and they cannot leave their houses. There is no other work.

What can we do to ensure that this kind of attack never happens again? We can pray for the strength as Christians to love those who think that they are our enemies. We can meet and learn about people of other faiths, so that we can know them as children of God and discover that peace is central to our faiths, especially to Christianity and Islam. We can give support to the programs and mission partners that feed the hungry, comfort the wounded, and seek justice for the oppressed.

If there are pictures of new bombs falling on Kabul or on the barren countryside of Afghanistan, please keep in mind the farmers without crops, the women who cannot leave their houses, and the unimaginable horror of innocent people with nowhere to get away from the destruction. It is outrageous and infuriating that their country could be attacked like that. It would be the most unlawful and unjust act to kill thousands of people because we are angry with their government.

Help us to stand in solidarity with all those affected by conflict—those who have lost homes, family members, livelihood, and community. We pray that they may still have hope and that they will feel God's presence in each other and in those who give them comfort. May God open our eyes to the suffering of people whom we see only in pictures but to whom we are connected through our common humanity, created in God's image.

Stephanie Spencer is program associate for the Southern Asia Office in Cleveland.

From the United Church of Christ Web site <www.ucc.org>, September 2001. Used by permission.

WE WHO ARE MANY ARE ONE BODY

The People of God Come Together

∾

For as in one body we have many
members and not all the members have
the same functions, so we, who are many,
are one body in Christ, and individually
we are members one of another.

—Romans 12:4–5

∾

N September 11, 2001, AMERICANS LEARNED IRREVOCABLY that they are truly part of a global community, no longer isolated from the prosaic violence and daily unrest suffered by other nations. In the days after the attacks on New York and Washington, many began to realize in a new way the fundamental interconnectedness of global politics, economics, history, and even religion. And some also began to understand the potential power of a common witness for peace, justice, and reconciliation.

Within the Christian community, response from around the globe was swift and universal. Letters and e-mail poured in to denominational and conciliar offices from Asia and South America, from Europe and the Pacific Rim; missionaries in the field passed along heartfelt condolences, as one reported, "like a fraternal hug, crossing borders and united in faith." Many of the letters expressed the abiding hope that, around the world, Christians could be united as human beings against terrorism and as people of faith in common witness to God's hope, even in the valley of the shadow of death.

A Prayer for Our Life and Our World

September 12, 2001

❀

KRISTEN HERZOG

WE BRING BEFORE YOU, O God, our trials and tears, our hopes and fears. We are shaken by the unspeakable cruelty of what human beings have done to innocent people in the name of faith, and yet we suffer from what is being done from our side to other innocents in the name of safety and freedom. We are confused about our loyalties and responsibilities, thinking about the leaders and fighters on all sides of the conflict, the refugees and prisoners, the wounded and the dying, the children and the aged. We know that our recent experiences of anxiety and terror are only shadows of what millions of people in other parts of the world have lived with on a daily basis. We ask your forgiveness for having neglected those who subsist on a dollar a day while we worry about our stock market losses. We are embarrassed that we fail in interpersonal as much as in international relationship and that our prejudices against other countries and religions simply reflect our failure to listen to those who are different from us in our families, our local communities, and our nation.

We bring it all before you, the horrible and the routine, the heartache of losses and the daily triumphs of survival and achievements; the helplessness of our efforts and the miracle of renewed energy. We ask for courage to speak the truth, for imagination to make peace while working for justice, for new eyes to see the beauty and fragility of our world, for wisdom to be faithful stewards of your creation. Make us aware that we are only small links in your great chain of grace that connects us with living beings of any nation, faith, and race as well as with generations before us and after us. Fill us with your Spirit that is as boundless as the air we breathe.

Keep before us the image of Jesus Christ who taught us to live like your trusting child while putting his life on the line for the truth of your peace. Amen.

From the United Church of Christ EKU Working Group resource, "You Gave the Weary Your Hand" (November 2001). Reprinted by permission.

MECC Letter on the Attack against the U.S.A.

September 12, 2001

❀

MIDDLE EAST COUNCIL OF CHURCHES

DEAR FRIENDS, Our Brothers and Sisters in Christ in the United States,

The grace of our Lord Jesus Christ, the Father's love and mercy, and solace of the Holy Spirit, the Comforter, surround and bear you up on this morning after the day of tragedy.

The world—we all—stopped, horrified. The massive scale of the violence, particularly in New York but also in Washington, has been beyond belief. Imagination cannot picture what may be its repercussions as anger yields to cries for vengeance. Almost instantly, the images flooded out over the TV networks, horrific descriptions over our radios. Where we were first touched was in our human soul. We were caught up in the agony of individuals amplified manifold. And words are not enough to describe this, even though that is all that we have at the moment.

I wish to express to our friends in the United States our profound condolences for the loss of loved ones. In gathering after gathering in America, Christians will lift up their hearts in prayer. We assure you that we, too, are gathering, and our prayers join yours. We ask for healing beyond understanding; we pray for courage beyond our outrage and fear. We ask for the grace, the steadfast poise of faith, to stand with integrity and minister in an ever-more dangerous world.

We are devastated by the bestiality that can infect ordinary human beings and transform them into mass murderers and deranged suicides. Evil raised its head. Its taunting must be resisted. Evil does not overcome evil; it augments it. Christ taught us that. The democratization of terror and violence on a massive scale points to a profound distortion in the human spirit of our times. And, as those who bear the Gospel of Peace, it is this distortion we must overcome. With you we mourn the innocent dead; we bewail our own loss of innocence, our loss of confidence, our loss of a sense of security. And we do so out of a Middle East that has known more than its fair share of death, disillusionment, and fear over all-too-many decades. But with you, too, we are determined that death shall have no dominion. Your hope and our hope will not be crushed.

In the name of all the member churches of the Middle East Council of Churches, in the name of our presidents and staff, I stretch out to you our love and compassion in Christ's name and for his sake. We break one bread and are one Body. Holding to that reality with a firm grip, you will rise above this tragic moment and, with you, we, too, will rise. Let us together seek the healing of the nations and overcome this and all evil with good.

In Christ's name and in his peace that passes understanding,

Rev. Riad Jarjour
General Secretary for the MECC

Reprinted by permission of the Middle East Council of Churches.

Dear Brothers and Sisters in Christ

Kirchenkanzlei, Berlin, September 13, 2001

❀

EVANGELICAL CHURCH OF THE UNION

GRACE TO YOU, and peace, from God, our Father, and the Lord Jesus Christ!

We, your brothers and sisters of the Evangelical Church of the Union, want to assure you that we are with you with our tears, out thoughts, and our prayers. We are united with you. United now in pain, grief, and helplessness. We pour out our hearts before God, turning to God seeking comfort, advice, and wisdom, since we are deeply hurt and scared. We are terrified watching television pictures. We cannot believe what we have seen— images burning in our hearts, impossible to forget. Again and again, we have to tell ourselves that this is neither science fiction nor a horror film but horrible reality.

Side-by-side, we stand with those who suffer. We think about the injured and those who have lost their loved ones and those who are still between hope and despair. Now, all Christians are asked to be witness of their hope. Christ calls us to be with those who mourn, with those who are lonely in their pain. In our churches, people gather in worship services, turning to the One who is as good as his words.

We feel the unity with you also through the presence of John Thomas and Peter Makari, who took part in services in Berlin and Potsdam. An ecumenical vigil in the Berlin Dom (cathedral), held seven hours after the first news reached the city, was overcrowded. Not only did many church officials and politicians take part, but also hundreds were standing outside in the rain, soothing their desperate souls by singing songs of peace. As we arrived the next morning to meet with the staff in the EKU Church Office to have a service together, we found greetings, words of comfort from other regional churches of the EKU.

The Church of Westphalia, where a UCC delegation from the Indiana-Kentucky Conference is visiting, donated a substantial sum towards the relief efforts of the UCC. Yesterday, in Potsdam, our guests took part in another service where an amazing number of firefighters were present. They wanted to express their particular sympathy and solidarity with their colleagues in New York City. Uncounted signs of solidarity: That is the living experience of what Full Communion-*Kirchengemeinschaft* means.

We have reminded ourselves of the hope that we have, the hope that we have to speak about. Even in such times, we are not lost. In Christ, we seek comfort and advice. He has overcome death, violence, and vengeance with his love . . . through his love even in deepest suffering and despair.

We pray with you for those who lost their lives as helpless victims and for those who have died in their attempt to save the lives of others. We pray for the government, that wisdom may govern them in their difficult decisions and that any efforts to establish peace throughout this world may be supported.

We are united with you in Christ. With Paul, we are convinced that "neither death, nor life, nor angels, nor rulers, nor things present, nor things to come, nor powers, nor height, nor depth, nor anything else in all creation, will be able to separate us from the love of God in Christ Jesus our Lord" (Rom. 8:38–39).

Yours in Christ,
Wilhelm Hueffmeier
President, EKU

A letter submitted to the Middle East and Europe Office, Partner Relations Ministry, Wider Church Ministries, A Covenanted Ministry of the United Church of Christ. Used by permission.

Letter from Istanbul, Turkey

❀

ALISON STENDAHL

SINCE TUESDAY, I have experienced a tremendous outpouring of love, sympathy, solidarity, and support. The Turkish people are crying with us. Turkish colleagues at school have been enveloping the American faculty, listening carefully with tears in their eyes to the various stories of those who had family members in Washington, D.C. and New York City. Muslims are saying that these acts of terrorism are not Islam. They fear that all Muslims will be labeled and condemned. The Turkish press, ranging from the most liberal to the Islamic conservatives, is united in its outrage and condemnations. In the *Turkiye* newspaper, a conservative Islamic newspaper, the following was written in both Turkish and English, "We condemn the acts of terrorism in the United States and offer our condolences to the American people." It spoke of how the Christian Armenian churches in Istanbul rang their bells, and it showed photos of people in Germany, Spain, Belgium, Bulgaria, and England sharing the pain of the American people. Europe came to a standstill for three minutes on Friday, a day that was a day of mourning not only for the U.S.A. but also for the entire world. People are standing united as human beings against terrorism, no matter their religion or ethnicity. Those who rejoice are few. I am pleased that so many people are cautioning the labeling of all Muslims as terrorists. I am ashamed of Americans who have attacked Islamic centers in the United States out of their anger and hurt, for this is no better than the terrorism they protest.

Turkey is a NATO country and a predominantly Muslim country. Prime Minister Ecevit has stated that Turkey will do what is necessary in this new war against terrorism. The message I wish for the U.S.A. churches to hear is that the American people are not alone and isolated. They need to see the love and support that surrounds them, even from Muslims and from people who do not agree with the U.S.A. foreign policy in the Middle East. The balances in the Middle East are delicate, and a great deal of thought needs to go into any actions.

For evil to exist, all it takes is for good to do nothing. —*Edmund Burke*

Perhaps the good have finally had it with the evil.
May God continue to walk with us through these difficult times.

Selam/Shalom

A Letter to Partner Churches in North America
and Related Missionary Personnel in Taiwan

September 12, 2001

❀

GENERAL ASSEMBLY OF THE PRESBYTERIAN CHURCH IN TAIWAN

DEAR FRIENDS,

Like the rest of the world since yesterday, we are trying to digest the news of the devastating terrorist attacks in the U.S.A. that have dominated our TV monitors and impacted our hearts—it is beyond comprehension. A tragedy of such magnitude—horrific for the victims, their families, and communities directly involved—cannot but also pierce the hearts of your entire nation and the entire world.

On behalf of the officers and constituent members of the Presbyterian Church in Taiwan, we convey our deep sorrow and express our sympathy to the victims, their families, to your people, the leaders of your government, your congregations, and, not forgetting the least among you, the children of your land.

For members of the ecumenical family, this horror brings into sharp focus the WCC theme and its commitment for the 2001–2010 Decade to Overcome Violence. Let this be a challenge for us to dedicate ourselves with renewed enthusiasm to strive for peace and justice by no violent means in our respective regions.

As an expression of our sympathy, compassion, and solidarity, the PCT has decided to provide immediately for our partner churches, PC (U.S.A.), PCA, and UCC/ Disciples of Christ, the amount of U.S. $3,000 to each church. Kindly let us know as soon as possible the bank details where the donations should be deposited for your respective denominational relief fund.

This morning, colleagues in the PCT General Assembly Office prayed for you— please be assured the prayers of your sisters and brothers in Taiwan will continue.

In the aftermath of the tragedies in New York and Washington and Pennsylvania, we bring before the Sovereign God:

the victims, those who grieve for their loved ones and for the people
   of your country
—Lord, embrace them in your arms and comfort them

the teams involved in the rescue efforts and emergency services
—Lord, give them courage and stamina in these immediate crucial hours

the children of your communities
—Lord, take away their fears that they may know security in your hands

the congregations of each of your denominations
—Lord, give them boldness to share the love and hope of Christ so those in
    pain may know healing and wholeness

the terrorist organizations
—Lord, may they be convicted by your grace and be accountable for their
    actions before God and international law

the president and leaders of your nation
—Lord, grant them your wisdom and strength to make responsible decisions

the leaders of all nations
—Lord, that they earnestly seek peaceful resolutions that will put an end
    to such needless, inhumane act of senseless terror

Lord in Your Mercy, hear our prayers, Amen.

William J. K. Lo
The Presbyterian Church in Taiwan

This letter was forwarded via e-mail from the general secretary of the Presbyterian Church in Taiwan to partner churches and missionaries in North America. Reprinted by permission.

Letter from the Justapaz

❀

MENNONITE CHURCH OF COLOMBIA

DEAR BELOVED SISTERS AND BROTHERS,

In this time of uncertainty and sadness due to the recent tragedy in the United States, we want you to know that we are accompanying you, extending our love and solidarity to our family in the North.

In a country where the fear, anguish, and pain of war are seemingly permanent, we understand your hurting. We share your grief, confusion, and incomprehension. We, too, abhor this war that takes us further from Jesus' principles of justice and peace.

We condemn this act of violence, just as we denounce all behavior stealing life, regardless of place or the nationality of the victims or the perpetrators. We, too, yearn for peace, the fruit of justice. The Holy Spirit has filled us with hope, and you have accompanied us with solidarity and love. We now offer our love and support to you, suffering with you in this dark moment.

We urge you to accompany and advise your government in the love of Jesus and principles of nonviolence, encouraging national leaders to respond in ways that will break this cycle of violence and not cause more suffering. We are praying for the presence of God's wisdom as you discern the direction you should take, as a church and as a nation.

This is an opportunity to evaluate the concepts of justice and reconciliation and reconfirm promises to nonviolence and the construction of peace. As seekers of light, we have the assurance that God will accompany us in these dark moments of pain and chaos.

A fraternal hug, crossing borders and united in faith.
Justapaz and the Justice and Peace Committee of the Colombian Mennonite Church

This e-mail was forwarded to Wider Church Ministries executives on September 14, 2001, from the Justice and Peace Council of Mennonite Church of Colombia. Reprinted by permission.

Kirchengemeinschaft in schwieriger Zeit

❁

Max Koranyi

WHEN I WATCHED—between two confirmation classes—the attack on the World Trade Center on September 11, I knew at once that this disaster would as well bring to fall the feeling of security in which I grew up in my country. In German history, there has never been a longer period of peace than the last fifty-six years. This time, it seemed to me, was coming to an end when thousands of people from a country to which I feel a close relationship were killed.

Before this terrible "Ground Zero" experience took place, the EKU/UCC working group had planned to hold its meeting in Andover Newton Theological School, close to Boston. It was totally understandable that many members didn't feel comfortable to use an airplane to come to the convention. Nevertheless, the EKU had already bought a ticket for me as chairman of our UCC-Forum in Berlin. And, as I was also asked to give the sermon on the day of dedicating the new church building of our partner congregation in Virginia Beach, Va., I finally decided to travel to the U.S.A. It wasn't an easy decision for my family and me. But the day before I flew to Boston, I got an e-mail from a member of the UCC from Texas telling me that especially in "such a time as this," we need each other in *Kirchengemeinschaft* more than ever, quoting the proverb: "A friend in need is a friend indeed." I know, of course, that one can't compare the situation or the persons who were involved, but nevertheless I was reminded of the time when Dietrich Bonhoeffer felt the call to travel from the United States to Germany, where he thought he was especially needed.

I've never regretted it for a single minute to have come to our friends of the UCC during a time when the bombing of Afghanistan began on October 7. When I arrived in Boston, I saw on my way to Andover Newton Theological School a church sign of a Lutheran church announcing the sermon for the next Sunday with the following words "Defy terror, live with courage, retaliate with love, return evil with good." And, at once, the most important issues of the UCC came to my mind, a church that has tried over decades to stay faithful to its call as a "just peace church." And during all the turmoil and threats, which were felt right there as well, I noticed a renewed upspring of the *Friedensbewegug*. Prof. Mark Burrows, who kindly picked me up at the airport, had sent me some e-mail, thus giving me the opportunity before our meeting to share some deep theological insights. He wrote: "The lasting peace we desire comes when we defeat the violent mind, not the violent body." And, he continued: "I do wonder what the world might look like if we took the war on poverty, on hunger and disease, as seriously as we seem to be taking this war on terrorism.

These were the issues that we discussed when I was privileged to meet with members of the working group who, despite all the threats, had come to meet me at Andover

Newton. One of the most touching moments was a discussion that took place with students of the seminary. One of the female students described the terrible situation of those people looking for a sign of a beloved one that was killed by the blast of the WTC. All the survivors were covered by gray dust, thereby no longer distinguishable by sex or race—being one human body suffering and grieving together the terrible loss. And then the story of the empty tomb came to her mind when the women looked for the body of Christ and couldn't find it any more and felt desperately lonely. They wanted to tell the grieving people that there would be the resurrection of the body, even if they couldn't find a single sign of the dead, because Jesus was called as the first one on to Eternal Life on Easter Sunday.

This sign of Eternal Life I was allowed to experience when I flew the following day to Virginia Beach, Va., to take part in the dedication ceremony of a newly built congregational center of the Tidewater UCC. For over ten years, my congregation in Königswinter, Germany, has developed a close relationship to this church by organizing a youth exchange. More than one hundred youth on both sides have already taken part in this wonderful, ecumenical experience, crossing borders and, thereby, crossing prejudices and minds as well. Now the time had come to dedicate a new building that the faithful congregation members had built just by themselves. In a way, I was reminded of the prophet Jeremiah when he told the people who were exiled to Babylon in a very difficult time, "Build houses and live in them!" So I tried to preach on this very Sunday, October 7, when the bombing of Afghanistan began: "Behold, the dwelling of God is with human beings." I told the parishioners that, in our church in Königswinter, two days after the attack, more than 120 people came to worship, prayed for peace, and lit candles in remembrance of those who suffered. I felt that this very worship service became part of the peace movement that again will be a special connecting link between our two churches. The decade to overcome violence has now got a very significant meaning for our common task. I'm sure we will rediscover the source of our belief: "Blessed are the peacemakers, for they shall be called children of God."

Pfr. Max Koranyi
Königswinter, Rhineland

Thoughts and Prayers to Friends of Sabeel in North America

❀

Sabeel Ecumenical Liberation Theology Center

Dear Brothers and Sisters,

We are stunned at the enormous tragedy that hit the U.S.A. yesterday and caused great suffering to the American people.

As we grieve the loss of so many lives, we share your sorrow, fear, and concern for your loved ones and all innocent people, victims of hatred and sick minds. The extent of the catastrophe reveals the vulnerability and weakness of human beings and governments in the face of terror.

As Palestinians who have been victims of terror, we are appalled at the reports of Palestinians celebrating your tragedy. Amidst all the pain and injustice that we have been living through the past year, we condemn all terrorist crimes that dehumanize and perpetrate evil. It is important to realize that, once more, the media is at work to divert attention from this terrible calamity by trying to find scapegoats to blame.

Now is the time to work with more determination to deal with the root causes that create violence, a violence that is consuming our world. It is the time to remember that only God is great. Let us pray that his love and mercy will comfort the bereaved, heal the injured, and help and guide leaders into making decisions that will avoid more suffering to humankind.

We pray for a just peace that will save our world.

Sabeel Ecumenical Liberation Theology Center

Reprinted by permission of SABEEL.

African Partners' Responses to 9-11

❀

AUTHOR UNKNOWN

THOUGH IT REMAINS UNCLEAR as to who actually masterminded and carried out the operation, we understand that this could have been caused by extreme elements within the Arab Muslim fraternity. If this is eventually confirmed, it reemphasizes the daunting task that we in Project for Christian Muslim Relations in **Africa** (PROCMURA) and our partners like you have in this delicate and sensitive vocation of fostering good relations between Christians and Muslims.

*I want to let you know that we are thinking of you all as American people, that we are praying for you and with you and that we admire the ministries in which you are involved in order to change this world and to make it a better place for all to live in. You all contributed in different ways to assist in the changes of the **South African** society, and, both as an individual and a South African, I want to express my gratitude and admiration for the extra miles that you walked with us in order to bring transformation.*

Please know that your brothers and sisters in Christ here in **Lesotho** are lifting up in our prayers the Disciples of Christ and the United Church of Christ and their members and all of the people of the U.S.A. As the Global Ministries of the Disciples and UCC stood with people of Lesotho during the riots and destruction that befell Lesotho in 1998, the LEC wishes your churches to know that it stands in solidarity with them during this crisis. As a small token of our support to those who have suffered so deeply from this attack, we are posting a cheque in the amount of U.S. $150.00 with the request that this be applied to relief efforts.

These are excerpts from various partner sources who e-mailed concerns to the Africa area executives in the week following September 11, 2001.

A Letter

❀

The Salvadoran Lutheran Church

WE ARE STUNNED AND MOVED, like all human beings now in this moment in history, that anyone would have the capacity to conceive of such abominable damage to inflict on other human beings. We are all children of God, and this is the beginning of the new millennium in which civilization is supposedly in unfettered advancement.

We are in solidarity with the suffering of so many innocent victims, their families, and the people of the United States in general. We pray that God will give you strength and the Spirit to maintain confidence in a better and more just world society. As Salvadorans, we know by experience the pain that the collective death of many brothers and sisters provokes. We would like to encourage you to glimpse the hope that is on the horizon.

The best honor we can give to so many innocent victims of this atrocious and condemnable attack should be the commitment to support the families and, above all, the children that might enjoy a climate of integral and complete liberty and security as well as respect for life.

Brothers and sisters, we are praying with you that tranquility will be reestablished and that the families who cry for their loved ones will be comforted. We pray that, with the help of God, you will have strength to overcome this hard trial on life's way.

We have asked our national churches and their respective communities of faith and life for their prayers for the victims and families of this horrendous nightmare, that God would help them to come through this to a more just global society in peace with all respect for life.

United in Christ, fraternally,
Matador Ernesto Gómez
Bishop

Ricardo Cornejo
Assistant to the Bishop

Jaime Dubon
Sister Parish Program

This was an e-mail message sent to the area office executive by the Bishop of the Salvadoran Lutheran Church. Reprinted by permission.

Our Prayers Are with You

❀

Korean Christian Church in Japan

Dear Rev. Zhu:

Today, as we learn more of the aftermath of the attacks on the U.S., we wish to let you know that you and our brothers and sisters in America are in our thoughts and prayers.

We feel angry to be helpless in the face of such unnecessary attacks on human life. At the same time, our hearts grieve for all those who are hurting, who are still awaiting information on loved ones, who have lost family members, and who have been eyewitnesses to the events that have been taking place. They are in the central focus of our prayers.

Additionally, we pray for the U.S. government and the people of America, that they may make wise decisions in the midst of great anger and distress. We pray also for our churches as they reach out to help people, that they may continue to bring God's comfort and strength in the midst of pain.

If there is anything that we, the Korean Christian Church in Japan, can do to assist you at this time, we would certainly be glad to do what we can to help.

In Christ,
Kang Young Il
KCCJ General Secretary

This letter was sent via e-mail to area office executives on September 11, 2001, by the KCCJ general secretary. Used by permission.

Concern about the Attacks on Afghanistan
by the United States of America and Its Allies

Jakarta, October 12, 2001

❦

EXECUTIVE BOARD OF THE COMMUNION OF CHURCHES IN INDONESIA

THE ATTACKS ON AFGHANISTAN by the U.S.A., England, and their allies since 7 October 2001, give great cause for concern and deserve our censure.

We fully support U.S. efforts to demand accountability of those who committed and of all parties responsible for the 11 September tragedy in New York and Washington. Terrorism in any form, particularly terrorism such as that against the WTC in New York and the Pentagon building in Washington, are not in accord with just and civilized humanity. Every person and every nation adhering to humanitarian values would have to reject such terrorist actions.

However, the attack on Afghanistan by the U.S.A. and her allies will cause another human tragedy, no less tragic than the human tragedy of 11 September. The innocent people of Afghanistan, who have suffered greatly as a result of the struggle for power within their country, will be subject to even greater suffering.

The Communion of Churches in Indonesia rejects any violence, particularly war, definitely. Any form of violence is not in accord with mankind's dignity, is a violation of human rights, never solves problems, but rather traps mankind in a vicious cycle of suffering.

Therefore, the Executive of the Indonesian Communion of Churches, which represents seventy-eight churches and their members, wishes to state that it:

Censures the attacks on Afghanistan by the United States, England, and their allies.

Requests the United States and her allies to immediately halt their attacks and use the channel of legal action to bring to account those responsible for the terrorist attacks on 11 September 2001 in New York and Washington.

Expresses its solidarity with the millions of Afghanistan people whose suffering has been exacerbated by these attacks.

Calls on all parties, including the Taliban authorities in Afghanistan, to cooperate in efforts to overcome international terrorism because terrorism in any form is a violation of just and civilized humanity.

Calls on all elements and groups within Indonesia to adopt a balanced viewpoint of the conflict between the United States and the Taliban authorities in Afghanistan. We understand that this conflict is not an interreligious conflict specifically between Islam and Christianity but a conflict between the United States and groups that she considers to be international terrorist organizations and also the powers which defend them.

Calls on all the Indonesian people to strive together to take concrete humanitarian action to help the Afghanistan people who have been experiencing a period of prolonged suffering.

Calls on all social and political forces within the Indonesian nation to adopt a wise and balanced attitude to the conflict between the United States and the Taliban in Afghanistan, not forgetting that Indonesia herself is currently struggling with all her might to free herself from the depths of a multidimensional crisis. The consolidation of the social and political strengths of this nation is needed in order to together overcome social, economic, and other problems that are burdening the lives of millions of Indonesians.

Asks the United Nations to include in its agenda a discussion of the demands of many nations, particularly developing nations, for relationships between nations characterized by greater justice for all.

Such is our appeal and our expression of concern. Thank you, and may God bless us all.

Natan Setiabudi
General Chairperson

Ishak P. Lambe'
General Secretary

This letter was sent via e-mail to area office executives on September 11, 2001. Used by permission.

WHAT ARE WE TO SAY ABOUT THESE THINGS?

Theological Reflections on September 11, 2001

*What then are we to say about
these things? . . . Who will separate us
from the love of Christ? Will hardship,
or distress, or persecution, or famine, or
nakedness, or peril, or sword? . . .
No, in all these things we are more than
conquerors through him who loved us.*

—Romans 8:31, 35, 37

*For now we see in a mirror, dimly,
but then we will see face to face. Now I
know only in part; then I will know fully,
even as I am fully known.*

—1 Corinthians 13:11–12

AFTER WORLD WAR II, IT WAS SAID, ALL REFLECTION ABOUT GOD must take the Holocaust into account. What kind of God allows millions of innocents to die? Where is God in the midst of unspeakable violence and suffering? And if God is hidden or absent or impotent in the face of undeniable evil, why should anyone worship or praise such a God?

Nearly three generations have passed since the end of World War II. Today's religious leaders know the Holocaust largely through books and occasional encounters with aging survivors. Imperceptibly, Christians, especially American Christians whose lives have for two centuries been free of the fear of external enemies, have become accustomed once again to a God whose largesse and protection seem unbounded. "God Bless America," they sang and meant it not as a supplication but as a statement of fact.

All this changed after September 11, 2001.

After September 11, many American Christians discovered a God they had not known before. When shock and horror and fear diminished, hard questions took their place. Some religious leaders offered easy answers. In the devastation of New York and Washington, they saw divine retribution for America's presumed social and political sins. Others avoided facile conclusions, arguing instead for the inadequacy of human words and thoughts to comprehend God's "unfathomable ways," but now we see as if in a mirror, dimly; now we can know only in part.

A year later, questions remain. But some things seem clearer now. Where was God on Tuesday, September 11? God was with the victims in their agony. God was with the rescue workers and medical technicians. God was with the grieving families and friends. And in the words of United Church of Christ minister Lourdino A. Yuzon, God is with us now if we seek God, "reminding us that for every Good Friday, there is a Resurrection Sunday, assuring us that our journey through the valley of suffering and death will lead us to life."

A New Hymn

❀

CARL DAW JR.

WHEN SUDDEN TERROR TEARS APART

C. M. Suggested tunes: Bangor, Detroit, or C. M. D. Suggested tune: Third Mode Melody

When sudden terror tears apart
the world we thought was ours,
we find how fragile strength can be,
how limited our powers.

As tower and fortress fall, we watch
with disbelieving stare
and numbly hear the anguished cries
that pierce the ash-filled air.

Yet most of all we are aware
of emptiness and void:
of lives cut short, of structures razed,
of confidence destroyed.

From this abyss of doubt and fear
we grope for words to pray,
and hear our stammering tongues embrace
a timeless Kyrie.

Have mercy, Lord, give strength and peace,
and make our courage great;
restrain our urge to seek revenge,
to turn our hurt to hate.

Help us to know your steadfast love,
your presence near as breath;
rekindle in our hearts the hope
of life that conquers death.

Carl Daw is executive director of the Hymn Society. His hymns appear in The New Century Hymnal. *Carl can be reached at Boston University School of Theology. To reach the Hymn Society call 1-800-THE HYMN or e-mail to <hymnsoc@bu.edu>.*

On Binding up Wounds and Resisting the Powers

❈

GABRIEL FACKRE

JESUS WEPT (Lk. 19:41). Tears rolled down the face of God for Jerusalem, and today God weeps for New York. Deity was there at Ground Zero. And we, too, are called to that place to participate in the sufferings of God (Dietrich Bonhoeffer). Where there is the slaughter of innocents and hurt of such magnitude, our first ministry is to bind up wounds and thereby keep company with Christ. And to reach out in compassion as well to Arabs—Arabs who are Muslims, Christians, and followers of other faiths. They and the other peoples of the Middle East and South Asia had no part in this atrocity and also suffer from unreasoning hate.

The response of the United Church of Christ so far has shown that it understands the call to minister to the neighbor in need. The outpouring of prayer and care has been overwhelming, moved by the love of God. But do we also know what to do with the wrath of God? One of our great United Church of Christ theologians of an earlier era was not so sure. H. Richard Niebuhr indicted liberal Protestantism for teaching "a God without wrath who brings humans without sin into a kingdom without judgment through a Christ without a cross."

"Judgment" here has to do with holding the perpetrators responsible for this atrocity. Their suicide bombing was not a passport to paradise but a passage to the Great Judgment where they will answer for their sin before a righteous God. And their sponsors will give an account as well to the world's community of conscience, gathering now to bring terrorism to justice. And what of our own share in the judgment of God for an American hubris so graphically symbolized by the Babel-like proportions of our towers? Are we free of all guilt of the horror that happened? What is it about us that evokes the hate of so many of the world's poor? Dare we listen to Jeremiah's thunderbolts as well as Jesus' weeping?

We must learn to put together both the tough and the tender love of God. We get some help from yet other forebears who had to work out a Christian response to the terrorists of their day. In 1941, the Reformed theologian Karl Barth wrote a letter to Christians in Great Britain as bombs were falling on their cities. He reminded them of Good Friday but also of Easter morning, when God's definitive answer to the world's crucifiers was Resurrection (Col. 2:15). That victory assures the coming of the final reign of God, where every flaw shall be mended and absolute justice done. Because Jesus Christ has risen from the dead, Barth wrote, "the world in which we live is no sinister wilderness where fate or chance hold sway, or where all sorts of 'principalities and powers' run riot unrestrained. . . . " That resurrection faith empowers us to "come to grips spiritedly and resolutely with these evil spirits." And he added that "we shall not regard this war . . . either as a crusade or as a war of religion . . . [but] as a large-scale police measure which has become absolutely necessary in order to repulse an active anarchism."*

Much to ponder here.

Reinhold Niebuhr, another United Church of Christ giant of that earlier day, also has some counsel for us. Like Jeremiah, he was unsparing in his criticism of his nation's arrogance. He called for penitence for our sins and urged the making of peace as our controlling vision. But he pressed home, as well, the distinction that had to be made between tyranny and democracy and the need to defend the legacy of freedom and justice for all from the perils of the hour.

Our challenge in a United Church of Christ that prides itself on being a "just peace church" (and rightly so) is to deepen the meaning of that self-definition. No peace is worth having that does not bring the guilty to justice and, thus, our mandate to "resist the powers of evil." We do so with penitence and a passion for peace, confident of God's presence in both trial and rejoicing and the coming of that Realm that has no end. And, with the reminder to ourselves that what counts most is the Word about who God is and what God does, more than preoccupation with who we are in our justice-doing and peace-making.

> Unless the Lord builds the house, those who build it labor in vain. Unless the
> Lord guards the city the guard keeps watch in vain —*Psalm 127:1*

*Quotations from Karl Barth, A *Letter to Great Britain from Switzerland* (London: Sheldon Press, 1941).

Gabriel Fackre is a former professor of theology at Andover Newton Theological School in Newton Centre, Massachusetts. Fackre is a founding member of Confessing Christ and one of the most distinguished ecumenical theologians in the United Church of Christ.

A speech delivered at a convocation at Andover Newton Theological School, Newton Centre, Massachusetts. Reprinted by permission.

A Reflection on a Just Peace Church Response to the September 11 Event

❀

ROSEMARY McCOMBS MAXEY

GAY McCORMICK of Westminster, Md., and I (from Dustin, Okla.) flew into San Jose Airport on Monday night ready to "take care of" my graduate-student son, Adrian, who was having his wisdom teeth removed. We had planned for him to need us just enough to warrant the trip, and we would have plenty of time left over to see and enjoy the sights of San Francisco. I also planned to put the finishing touches on a sermon to be delivered on Sunday, September 16.

The lectionary readings, particularly the Jeremiah writings, were ripe with possibilities for raining down the wrath of God on an unsuspecting congregation. The poems and oracles, often spoken in God's voice, condemn the arrogance, idolatry, violence, and unfaithfulness of God's people and nations. Then, in mercy, God calls for their return to God's self. Jeremiah shows us the foolishness of nations of people who made wrong choices, left behind the wrong models for problem solving, and even with brief moments of repentance, they returned to offer more wrong choices and models. "When will they AND WE ever learn?" I had planned to rhetorically ask the Fellowship Congregational United Church of Christ of Tulsa, Oklahoma.

But Tuesday morning, September 11, changed my thoughts and plans. In the unbelievable moments of that morning, all the vigor of the prophetic voice crumbled and gave way to tears of grief and feelings of helplessness. The movement from viewing the way God's world ought to be to the way God's world really is was swift and fearsome. The poems and oracles of Jeremiah seem to come to pass here and now.

What is a "just peace church" response to the tragedies of September 11, 2001? What, specifically, is my just peace response to God, my neighbor, and to myself? How may I join with others of my faith to denounce the terrors of evil, and how may I bring myself to participate in acts of justice so that healing and peace may become real?

In the immediacy of the week following September 11, I was grateful for God's presence made visible through my son, my trusted friend, and two young-adult friends from my former parish, and my son's roommate. I was thankful for the wireless connections that put me in touch back home with family and friends and for my faith communities. God said, "For now, this is your home and you have all that you need in the way of friends right here. And, you have work to do." In good and holy company, it was up to me to muddle through my thoughts and fears.

The importance of being connected with loved ones and people of faith cannot be overstated. It allows space for necessary lamentation. To rage and writhe with anguish is not due to a lack of faith in God or an act to blame God, but, rather, it brings people of faith to the place where we have been before—surviving violence, disaster, and sorrow together. Necessary lamentation is to grieve and still know that God cares. God who receives the full range of our anguish can be trusted with our grief.

As we watched people from around the world weeping with us, the global community, in its way, expressed its lamentation. My mother's pastor said in his sermon, "As I watched the faces of all the crying people, I thought I am being shown how it is when God cries." God cries, and God calls us to be close.

While the necessary lamenting is being done, the movement to testify to God's justice is coming due. For the just peace church member, there is more than one way to express God's justice. Some dig back into the roots of their faith to share with others in order to give and receive sustenance, solace, and wisdom. Others express in words, perhaps in Jeremiah's words, the need to restrain a nation that is quick to respond with vengeance. Still others will seek to understand what is beneath the hatred toward our nation and contemplate solutions. And, some will want to do something positive to show victims that they are not alone and not without means. Perhaps some will tend to the ordinary in their communities and churches, where the poor continue to live and have unmet needs. They will speak words of peace with their neighbors. Whichever route or plan we may take, collectively, our just peace responses will be those that do not engender more hatred and more violence anywhere.

In many American Indian cultures, warriors are often quoted as saying, "Vengeance is in my head, but peace is on my heart." In the early Muscogee (Creek) Confederacy of Alabama, Georgia, and Northern Florida, settlements were called "War Towns" and "Peace Towns," each with specific assignments for the well-being of the people. They were to be so closely intertwined that one did not declare war without the consent of the peace town, and the peace town did not close its eyes to the necessity of war to eradicate evil. In retrospect, one would know that the ideal was not allowed to come to fruition. Nations that rely solely on their rational "heads" don't often listen to the longings of their hearts, but it takes both to evoke and sustain justice.

Vengeance kills and diminishes all of us. Justice is healing, equalizing, and stabilizing. In this nation's context, justice is illusive and challenges us to recognize our nation's vulnerabilities as the same as those of Jeremiah's time. The just peace invitation is to make the right choices—to lament, to pray, to act, and to unite against the bitter fruits of division, hatred, and violence. Our soul-searching and plans of action would bring us to God, who can direct our paths to justice.

When I came home from my trip, my mother, Aunt Martha, and I reminisced about our trip to the top of the World Trade Center in 1979. We had spoken our Muscogee (Creek) language up there, adding it to the many other languages being spoken that day. My spouse and I reread our friend Ira Zepp's book called *A Muslim Primer: A Beginner's Guide to Islam.* I thought about Dale Bishop's article, "What Shall We Say about These Things?" Dale reflects on stands he has taken regarding the Middle East, leading in matters of justice for Palestinians, ending sanctions against Iraq, and other matters. "How could these people attack my city?" he asks. Many of us in the United Church of Christ have followed Dale's and others' leadership in supporting similar stands—our attempts at being faithful. My reminiscence, readings, and thoughts lead to prayers, prayers for my community and prayers for the global community.

In the sacred web of life, we are connected to people around the world who are our neighbors. It is important to care about them. My responsibility is to acknowledge the connections and speak and act boldly regarding issues that make for peace with justice.

In addition to praying my own thoughts and petitions, I have read the prayers of others, particularly those offered by our United Church of Christ leaders, and those from Jewish and Islamic faiths. What I am most drawn to are the combined prayers of Rev. Kay Besslor Northcutt, a Disciples pastor, and Rev. Leslie Penrose, pastor of the Community of Hope UCC in Tulsa. (By the way, Leslie was the one who preached at Fellowship in Tulsa when I could not get back in time for the service.)

> Abiding God, you dwell in our midst and gather our prayers into your life. In confidence and trust, we pray together for your broken and hurting world. You are with us in our knowing and our not knowing, our faith and our fear, in our living and our dying. Receive our prayers . . .
>
> For those who have died, and the loved ones who mourn them,
>
> For those who are injured or missing, and for those who wait hoping against hope,
>
> For rescue workers, doctors, and nurses as they search for life,
>
> For priests and rabbis, pastors and imams as they hear the laments.
>
> God of Abraham, Jesus, and Muhammad, you have birthed many people in many lands, gifted us with many tongues, and nurtured us with many faiths. Find us together this day with your extravagant grace. Lavish it on us and make of us one kin-dome, one world of shalom, of salaam, of peace. We give thanks, O God, for the words of comfort and solidarity that have come to us from around the world—we are strengthened by them. We lift to you those families in other nations who lost loved ones in this tragedy . . . and we pray this day, O God, for the men, women, and children of Afghanistan who must now add the fear of bombs to lives already torn by war and burdened by oppression.
>
> God of struggle, help us this day to offer prayers for those who committed these acts of violence. Even in death, we ask that you redeem them from the pit of hate and pain deep enough to lead them to become agents of unspeakable suffering.
>
> Seeking God, we open to you the dark corners within us where our deepest hungers, our unspoken fears, our feelings of rage, our need for someone to blame smolder just below the surface. Fill us with the light of your faithful assurance. Do not let grief or fear distort our vision or harden our hearts. In the days and months ahead, encourage our sometimes hesitant and wavering struggle to be faithful. Sustain us when the journey seems long, and we haven't enough resources to go it alone.
>
> Carve our names on your hand, O God, and dwell in our midst. Be our God and make of us your people as we pray now with Jesus and one another. Amen.

Rosemary McCombs Maxey is the executive director of the Council for American Indian Ministry.

From the United Church of Christ Web site <www.ucc.org>, September 2001. Reprinted by permission.

A Prayer for God's People in Time of Tragedy and Sorrow

❀

ROBERT G. HUNSICKER

ALMIGHTY AND ETERNAL GOD, great in power and even greater in mercy and compassion, whose love extends to the very ends of the earth, hear us as we bring to you our own needs and the needs of all who are suffering in our weary and troubled world:

For all whose hearts are heavy with grief and sorrow and especially for the families of those whose lives have been lost in the tragic events of September, we pray.

Lord, have mercy and grant us your peace.

For the leaders of our nation and of the nations of the world, that the day will come soon when all weapons of destruction are remolded into tools for peace and justice, we pray.

Lord, have mercy and grant us your peace.

For those engaged in ministries of reconciliation; for persons who are struggling to overcome the prejudice and hatred that so long have divided your people, we pray.

Lord, have mercy and grant us your peace.

For all who live in fear, fear of an uncertain future, fear of dying, we pray.

Lord, have mercy and grant us your peace.

For those in our own country and abroad who are experiencing hunger, that we be aroused from our indifference to their suffering and pain, we pray.

Lord, have mercy and grant us your peace.

For each of us and for all who have been baptized into the faith and family of Christ, that through us the light of Christ's presence illumine the dark places of the earth, we pray: **Lord, have mercy and grant us your peace.**

Through him who has come into our world that all your children may have life abundant, and who has taught us to pray:

Our Father in heaven, hallowed be your name. Your kingdom come; your will be done on earth as it is in heaven. Give us this day our daily bread and forgive us our sins as we forgive those who sin against us. Save us from the time of trial and deliver us from evil. For the kingdom, the power, and the glory are yours, now and forever. Amen.

Rev. Robert G. Hunsicker is pastor at St. Andrew United Church of Christ, Lancaster, Pennsylvania.

From the United Church of Christ EKU Working Group resource, "You Gave the Weary Your Hand" (November 2001). Reprinted by permission.

The Problem of Evil in the World

❀

LOURDINO A. YUZON

WHERE WAS GOD last Tuesday? God was with the victims, bearing with them their burden of fear, hopelessness, despair, agony, anger, pain, and death. God was with the firemen, policemen, rescue workers, and with doctors and nurses ministering to the injured. God is now with all people of goodwill, praying for the victims and their bereaved loved ones. God is with all those involved in a concerted effort to wage "war" against terrorism, reminding them of the need to take the high moral ground and opt for an action strategy that precludes the use of evil means that we deplore. God is with those who grieve over their irreparable loss, listening to their cries of anger, sorrow, despair, and hopelessness, always reminding them that God will not forsake or forget them. God is with this sorrowing nation, bringing healing and restoring wholeness to its severely wounded spirit. God is now with those terrorists, not to bless but to judge and give them their due. God is with us, reminding us that for every Good Friday, there is a Resurrection Sunday, assuring us that our journey through the valley of suffering and death will lead us to life in all of its God-given glory. God is with us, saying that it is not evil but God's absolute power of goodness, love, and life that will ultimately prevail.

In this moment, when our spirits are baptized by a baptism of fire, let us, with unshakable faith, steadfastly hold onto God's love that will not let us go. As St. Paul eloquently puts it, "I am convinced that neither death, nor life, nor angels, nor rulers, nor things present, nor things to come, nor powers, nor height, nor depth, nor anything else in all creation, will be able to separate us from the love of God in Christ Jesus our Lord" (Rom. 8:38–39).

Lourdino A. Yuzon is from Cosmopolitan United Church of Christ, Carrollton, Texas.

A sermon segment submitted for the United Church of Christ Web site <www.ucc.org>, September 16, 2001. Used by permission.

A Truth-Telling Comfort

❀

WALTER BRUEGGEMANN

THE EVENTS OF SEPTEMBER 11, 2001 (the bombings in New York City and Washington, D.C.) evoke for me the sobering verdict of Karl Barth:

> As ministers we ought to speak of God. We are human, however, and so cannot speak of God. We ought therefore to recognize both our obligation and our inability and by that very recognition give God the glory (*The Word of God and the Word of Man*, 186).

This surely is the perplexity in which pastors of the church find themselves always but intensely so in the face of that ominous happening. Of course, I have no warrant to speak beyond that of every sister and brother in ministry to speak when we cannot; but like every brother and sister in ministry, I have some obligation to try.

I.

The first word to be spoken in and by the church of course concerns *grief and comfort* over the insane loss of life that is, in the countless concrete cases, completely nonsensical. The grief is about loss, more so about meaningless, violent loss, and it must be uttered deep and loud and long and not quenched soon. I suspect that the church will be driven to texts of sadness such as it has not "needed" for a long time. The grief surely concerns personal loss. For this, a series of lament psalms provide a powerful script.

But the loss, beyond the personal, is a systemic shattering, a new public sense of vulnerability and outrage, an abrupt subverting of our shared sense that we in the U.S. are somehow immune from the rage of the world. There is currently great attention to "Lament Psalms" as they function in "pastoral care," an immense gain in church practice. Not so much noticed, however, are "communal laments" (such as Pss. 74 and 79) that bespeak the shattering of the most elemental public symbols of coherence and meaning, in the Old Testament embodied in the Jerusalem temple. This public dimension of grief is deep underneath personal loss and, for the most part, not easily articulated among us. But grief will not be worked well or adequately until attention goes underneath the personal to the public and communal. My expectation is that pastors, liturgical and pastoral, must need to provide opportunity and script for lament and complaint and grief for a long time. No second maneuver after grief shall be permitted to crowd in on this raw, elemental requirement.

The full voice of grief is to be matched, in pastoral attentiveness, by the *enactment of comfort* that seeks to meet grief. That comfort, of course, begins in bodily contact, but eventually we must speak about the God of all comfort beyond our feeble but indispensable personal offer of comfort. I suspect that in our effort to speak credible comfort, we will be driven back to Easter seriousness, an Easter claim that has not been very serious or even credible in much of our bourgeois self-sufficiency. The claim on which everything rests for us, however, is that the God of the gospel has rendered impotent "the last enemy" who can no longer rob us of life with the God of whom Paul affirms:

> For I am sure that neither death, nor life, nor angels, nor rulers, nor things present, nor things to come, nor powers, nor height, nor depth, nor anything else in all creation, will be able to separate us from the love of God in Christ Jesus our Lord. (Rom. 8:38–39).

We pastors utter these words almost every time there is a funeral. But now, I suspect, we will be tested by this required Easter utterance. On the one hand, we will be tested to see if we subscribe enough ourselves to say it; on the other, we are challenged to make sure that the affirmation is not glib in its failure to credit the durability of Friday and the permeability of Saturday, the power of which is not fully sated by Sunday morning. Church people will be helped by the affirmation that the anguish of Friday and Saturday persists, as we know in our own experience.

Grief and comfort come first and are the peculiar work of the believing community. For it is the comfort out beyond our management, the reality of God, that makes grief without protective denial possible. It is now frequently said that the U.S. church is "theologically soft" on the things that count. Now we shall see. We shall variously find out for ourselves in the dark silent hour of pastoral resolve.

II.

Beyond that obvious but urgent pastoral task that is entrusted peculiarly to such as us, we are drawn back to first questions by *the power of negation*, the kind of question that we often need not face. President Bush has said in response to the disaster, "Our nation has seen evil." He, of course, did not exposit his use of the word "evil," but his usage has given me pause. Most likely the president referred to the "evil persons" who committed this act of brutality, and that dimension of evil is not to be discounted.

But for pastors, the term "evil" evokes more and is not easily contained in human explanations about particular sins enacted by human agents. For "evil" draws us beyond "bad deeds" to cosmic questions. Very much Christian triumphalism claims easily that God in Jesus—at Easter—has eliminated the cosmic power of negation. Barth, however, has written of the durable power of "nothingness," and almost all of us are familiar with Cullman's suggestive notion about the continued threat of the enemy between D-Day and VE-Day. More recently, John Levenson, a Jewish interpreter, has shown that, in the Hebrew Bible, evil as a cosmic force persists, made visible in concrete acts but not contained in or reduced to visible acts. Evil persists in a powerful way in defiance of the will of the creator.

So what shall we tell our children? Perhaps we will have learned enough from the Jewish Holocaust to refrain from any glib triumphalism in order to affirm that God's crucified way in the world continues to be vulnerable and at risk from the demonic forces that may be in a last gasp, but in a powerful last gasp. Our children, so protected and privileged, may need to be delivered from romantic innocence to recognize that we live in a profoundly contested world, contested all the way down between God's good will and the deathliness of evil. Our commitment in the thick contest, moreover, matters, so that when we sign on (in baptism), we join the contest as partisans of the Vulnerable One and join the at-risk vocation that is the God-willed future of the world.

III.

Finally, of course, pastors with a cunning sense of good timing will eventually have to raise questions about U.S. policy and U.S. entanglement in the spiral of violence that continues to escalate. Much of popular opinion, reinforced by official posturing, acts as though Reinhold Niebuhr had never spoken about U.S. innocence and self-righteousness. The huge temptation for "Christian America" is to imagine that the U.S. is a righteous empire that endlessly does good around the world, comfortably portrayed in Manichean categories of good and evil. Such knee-jerk response to the crisis traffics in a combination of chauvinism and unreflective Christian triumphalism that refuses to think systemically about the U.S. as the international bully that continues to enact and embody the "Christian West" against non-Christian societies with its huge economic leverage and with immense, unrivaled military power. And with the gospel of Western globalism, the U.S. is passionately committed to override the fabric of any other kind of culture.

The prophetic task surely has never been more problematic for us than in this issue. The old texts articulate the stunning claim that God can indeed critique and move against God's own chosen people. The simple prophetic articulation by itself is too raw and must be accompanied by patient education in systemic analysis of power, an analysis known and implied in the prophetic texts but seldom made explicit.

There will be, to be sure, little patience among us for such systemic analysis, and pastors should not, in my judgment, resort to this second task too soon. But if pastors eventually settle only for interpersonal "grief and comfort," the deep issues of U.S. militarism in the service of U.S. consumerism will go unexplored, because there is almost nobody else for such analysis and such utterance.

This is a moment in which the pastors of the church might together—liberal and conservative—move out of deathly intramural spats to face big questions about good and evil and about our U.S. location in the midst of it all. Pastors who face such questions will be engaged in deep questions of their own faith. Pastors who face such questions will be beleaguered, because a triumphant society does not relish truth telling.

It occurs to me that Paul's lyrical declaration about ministry, so popular in more-or-less innocent ordination sermons, is a moving resource for today:

> We are afflicted in every way, but not crushed; perplexed, but not driven to despair, persecuted, but not forsaken; struck down, but not destroyed; always carrying in the body the death of Jesus, so that the life of Jesus may also be made visible in our bodies. (2 Cor. 4:8–10).

As you know, Paul concludes: "Therefore we do not lose heart" (v. 16). The heartless evils of September 11 could cause loss of heart. But our heart is set elsewhere in joy and freedom, in grace and in truth telling about the God of all truth.

I suggest that there are a series of important pastoral tasks concerning a) grief, b) comfort, c) cosmic evil, and d) social analysis. The evils of yesterday create a new context for priority. The rawness will make for careful alternative listening, because the word the church has now to speak matters enormously. Having said that, I finish by insisting, yet again, that the first task is grief, grief to be done long and well before anything else.

Walter Brueggemann teaches at Columbia Theological Seminary.

Psalm 46

Antiphonal Version

❀

MARY SUSAN GAST

Leader: God is for us refuge and strength

People: An ever-present help in trouble

Leader: Therefore we will not fear, though the earth should crumble,

People: Though the mountains shake in the heart of the sea:

Leader: Though its waters roar and foam,

People: And the mountains tremble with the surging.

Leader: There is a river whose streams delight the city of God, the holy habitation of the Most High.

People: God is present in the midst of the city;

Leader: It will not fall;

People: God will help it when the morning dawns.

Leader: The nations are in an uproar,

People: Governments totter;

Leader: The voice of The Holy One issues forth,

People: Earth yields.

Leader: The Almighty is with us;

People: The God of or ancestors is our protection.

Leader: Come, see what God does.

People: Does the Most High cause devastation on the earth?

Leader: No! God makes wars cease to the end of the earth; Breaking the bow, and shattering the spear;

People: Burning the shields with fire.

Leader: "Throw down your weapons and know that I am God!

People: "I reign most high among the nations,

Leader: "I am sovereign in the earth."

People: God Almighty is with us;

Leader: The God of our ancestors is our security.

Mary Susan Gast is the Conference minister for the Northern California-Nevada Conference.

From the United Church of Christ Web site <www.ucc.org>, September 2001. Used by permission.

A Time for Hope

❀

OTIS YOUNG

Scriptures: Romans 8:28, 31, 35, 37–39

ON TUESDAY MORNING, September 11, 2001, the people in our country and around the world were surprised and shocked by the terrorists' attack on the World Trade Center in New York City, the Pentagon in Washington, D.C., and the untold number of deaths and injuries these attacks caused. Added to this tragedy were the commercial airline planes that were used in the destruction and the lives of the people lost on those airplanes. The suffering and anguish is multiplied because of the torment this brings to the family members, friends, and coworkers of those who were injured and who died and, indeed, each one of us, whether or not we had a relative, friend, or coworker directly involved. We are in mourning, filled with rage; we are angry, anxious, afraid, and puzzled.

The deaths of so many innocent people raises all kinds of questions in our minds. Why do human beings do such things? What purpose does it serve? How can such acts of terrorism be prevented in the future? And the old nagging question for religious people is always there: "How can a good and loving God allow such things to happen to innocent people?" Where is God in such events?

There are no completely satisfying, simple, or instant answers to these and the many other questions we have. What we can do is turn to our faith and try to determine what guidance and direction it has to offer for us as individuals and as a nation. After much study and prayer during the days and nights since the events of September 11, here is what I believe our faith has to offer in terms of guidance, strength, and hope.

First and foremost: The Psalmist wrote years ago, "God is our refuge and strength, a very present help in trouble; therefore we will not fear though the earth should change; though the mountains shake in the heart of the sea; though its waters roar and foam; though the mountains tremble with its tumult." For me, personally, this means that my ultimate faith in the goodness and power of God continues. It doesn't answer all my questions. It doesn't mean that all my fears have magically gone away. It doesn't mean that I can make sense out of this mess. I sometimes wonder, as Jesus did, and as the Psalmist also wrote, "My God, My God, why have you forsaken me?" Even when I am uttering these words, I am expressing my faith in God.

Second, such events as the one on September 11 remind us that in spite of the goodness and power of God, we live in a world where the power of evil is still at work in some surprising and unexpected places. Not only is life in this world difficult and complex, it is also precarious. Sometimes when we think we are the safest, evil appears so that death and suffering come in unexpected ways.

Third, our faith cautions us, in such evil situations, not to panic so that we lose control. Panic can also cause us to quickly try to solve the problem with simple and, therefore, dangerous solutions that can, in many cases, only make the problem worse. In one of his most revealing parables, Jesus cautions us not to try to weed out the evil too quickly and thoughtlessly lest we destroy the good along with the evil or even, in some cases, give the evil more power.

I am convinced that justice will prevail; the evildoers will be caught. At the same time, the Bible cautions us to remember that the evil that was in them is still at work in many places. Good ideas and evil ideas are not killed by killing the people who harbor them. I am comforted by the way our governmental leaders, from the president on down, are dealing with the problems that face us. They are taking the necessary precautions but without a sense of panic.

What, then, on the positive side, are some things we can do as people of faith and as good citizens in a free country? Why have I given this sermon the title, "A Time for Hope"?

First of all, we can give thanks and continue to be grateful that we live in a nation where, in spite of such violent and evil actions, orderliness prevails. That's why it is a time for hope. I am overwhelmed and continue to be impressed with the outpouring of help and support for the victims and their families, from all over the country.

I am impressed with and thankful for the speed and efficiency with which our various arms of government responded and are still responding. In recent years, there have been too many people saying, "Can you name any one thing the government does well?" Even before this tragedy, I could have enumerated a long list, and now the list is longer.

I am thankful for the order-creating function of government in our free society, especially in such situations as we now face. I believe that, in the deepest sense as the Bible reminds us, that government officials and civil workers, whether they are appointed or elected, are to be seen as ministers of God. It is a high calling to be in public service, whether it be as a police officer, a firefighter, a public-school teacher, an Internal Revenue Service employee, or as a governor or the president.

All of these are reasons that cause me to believe that this is a time for hope, in spite of the tragedy and suffering that is present.

In the second place, it is time for hope because we believe in a God of hope. The Bible is, above everything else, a book filled with hope. It is filled with hope in this present world and in the future.

In the Hebrew Scriptures, which we call the Old Testament, the people of Israel continue to maintain their hope despite the many catastrophes in their history. Life was frequently difficult, but hope survived. The people of God continued to believe that tomorrow can be better than today. Throughout history, people of faith have had to struggle with continuous attacks of hopelessness, attacks against the faith that life has meaning even in the midst of tragedy and despair. The main character trait that separates a terrorist from the rest of us is that the terrorist is a person without hope. He or she only finds temporary hope in the suicidal killing of those believed to be the enemy, so that the reward is only in a life after this life.

For those of us who want to find hope in this life, in the present, and in the future, we begin to create the conditions under which hope can grow, and we openly and honestly talk about and face our fears and despairs with one another. Hope is what is still there when all our worst fears have been realized and faced.

That's what M. Scott Peck was saying in the opening paragraph of his book, *The Road Less Traveled*. He begins by saying, "Life is difficult." Then he goes on to say that once we truly know life is difficult, we can begin to transcend it. We can move beyond it.

The biblical stories contradict our prevalent impression that hope is dependent on hopeful circumstances. True hope is not like a thermometer, so that when conditions look hopeful, our hope rises, or when conditions are bad, our hope goes down.

The biblical foundation of hope is frequently suffering or trouble, not good times. From that we build endurance; out of that we build character, and from that we discover God's spiritual gift of hope. All of us know that we do not gain endurance from facing easy situations but from adversity. It is through meeting adversity that we build endurance and character and become the kind of people who can confront even desperate situations with hope.

Hope is not a mood but a quality of character called out from within us when needed.

That deep hope is based on our faith that God is in ultimate control of the creation and that, in the long run, in spite of setbacks, in spite of terrorists' attacks, God's will be done. There are seeds of this hope not only in the biblical narratives but also in a study of history.

Some years ago, a student of Charles Beard, the historian, asked him to put the principles that he had learned over a lifetime of historical study into a few brief statements. After some thought, he offered these four statements that are filled with hope:

1. The mills of God grind slowly, but they grind exceedingly fine.
2. Whom God would destroy, God first makes mad with power.
3. The bee fertilizes the flower it robs.
4. When it is dark enough, you can see the stars.

In the Hebrew Scriptures, the prophet Jeremiah demonstrated to the people of Israel what hope is all about. The enemy was at the gate of Jerusalem. The city was about to fall. The people were hungry and sick. Jeremiah himself was in jail. Yet under these seemingly hopeless conditions, Jeremiah bought a field as a sign of his confidence that this people, this world, had a future under God.

Jeremiah could take this action because he believed this is God's creation and that being so, it is never hopeless.

For us, you can be sure that the stock markets will reopen. Like Jeremiah, you and I will again invest in the future of this country. Tomorrow will be better than today. Over the long stretch of history, God's will not only will be done but is being done even in the midst of present circumstances, if not by us, then in spite of us.

You will also see this as a time for hope when you realize that the goal of creation under God is not some final stage of perfection but, rather, the creation of what is possible for humankind in each particular stage of history; and it is the struggle against the forces of evil, old ones and new ones, that arise in each period of history in a new way.

There have been and will continue to be victories as well as defeats in these struggles. But every victory, every particular progress from injustice to more justice, from suffering to more happiness, from hostility to more peace, from separation to more unity, anywhere in this world is another glimpse of the reign of God at work in time and space. It is, in the language of the Bible, the continual coming of the reign of God among us.

The reign of God does not come in one dramatic event sometime in the future. It is coming here and now in every act of love, in every manifestation of truth, in every moment of joy, in every experience of the holy. Our hope, then, is not in some final victory of God in the distant future but in the here and now, whenever and wherever the Eternal appears in time and history.

It helps to strengthen my hope when I remember that the power of God is found in the courage of human beings to stand up for human dignity, no matter what the odds. It helps strengthen my hope when I remember that God is not found only in happy endings or in one lifetime. Some problems are too grave to be solved that quickly and easily. It is God who links one lifetime to another, who joins one heroic sacrifice to another, until justice is established. My friends, that's why this time is a time for hope. Amen.

Let us pray.

Almighty God, whose love is everlasting and whose power endures throughout all generations, we remember in our prayers, your servants, the president of the United States, the governor of this state, and all others in authority. Fill them with the spirit of wisdom, goodness and truth, and so rule their hearts and bless their endeavors that law and order, justice and peace, may everywhere prevail. Preserve us from national sins and corruption. Make us strong and great in the fear of God and in the love of righteousness, reverent in the use of freedom, just in the exercise of power, and generous in the protection of the helpless so that we may become a blessing to all nations. Amen.

Otis Young is pastor of First-Plymouth Church, Lincoln, Nebraska.

This sermon was delivered by Otis Young at First-Plymouth Church, Lincoln, Nebraska, September 16, 2001. Reprinted by permission.

For Prayers in Silence

❁

KARL K. WHITEMAN

AT A MOMENT OF SUCH TRAGEDY and the terror of the last few days, images and emotions either freeze in our hearts or change with rapid-fire succession. Rather than filling prayers with predetermined words, invite people into silence. In the silence, images and emotions will arise before God. At intervals during the silence, you may ring a chime or suggest the following response.

One: God in your mercy,
People: send your holy peace.

The passing of Christ's peace may be a fitting conclusion to the prayers in silence.

In this time of great grief, sorrow, uncertainty,
and confusion around the world,
Almighty God, we gather our hearts and minds in prayer,
asking for your mercy, strength, and comfort for all those who suffer
from the terrible tragedy that has occurred
in New York City, Washington, D.C., and the plane crash in Pennsylvania.
Our hearts are open to all those who have been personally affected by this great tragedy.
We pray for wisdom, comfort, and healing.
Direct the actions of national and international leaders
not only in their efforts to seek justice for those responsible,
but also that they may help find new and better ways
to make our world safe for all—free from such senseless violence.
May we know in our hearts that you,
O God, are in control and your Word is still true.
Just and righteous God, we pray this
in the name of Jesus, the Prince of Peace,
and in the power of the Holy Spirit,
who comforts and strengthen us in our times of need. Amen.

Karl K. Whiteman is the liaison pastor for Micronesia and the Marshall Islands,
Common Global Ministries of the United Church of Christ and the Christian Church,
(Disciples of Christ) presently based in Pohnpei.

Prayer sent via e-mail to area executives, September 11, 2001. Reprinted by permission.

Prayer for the World

❀

LESLIE HOFFMAN

GIVE US COURAGE, O Lord, to stand up and be counted,
to stand up for those who cannot stand up for themselves,
to stand up for ourselves when it is needful for us to do so.
Let us fear nothing more than we fear you.
Let us love nothing more than we love you,
for thus we shall fear nothing also.
Let us have no other God before you,
whether nation or part or state or church.
Let us seek no other peace but the peace that is yours,
and make us its instruments,
opening our eyes and our ears and our hearts,
so that we should know always what work of peace we may do for you.

Leslie Hoffman is a twenty-year-old student at Ursinus College, Collegeville, Pennsylvania.

God Is Their Refuge

September 16, 2001

❁

PAUL TELLSTRÖM

HEBREW TESTAMENT READING: Psalm 46; GOSPEL READING: Luke 15:1–10

WHAT SCRIPTURE COMES TO MIND to help us, to give strength to us who have watched the disasters unfold in the days that have passed? There are so many times when I turn to the Forty-sixth Psalm, and I turn to it again as I have all week:

> God is our refuge and our strength, a very present help in time of trouble. Therefore, we will not fear though the earth be removed, and though the mountains be carried into the midst of the sea; though the waters be troubled, though the mountains shake with the swelling thereof. The Lord of Hosts is with us, God is our refuge. God makes wars to *cease* unto the ends of the earth. Be still, and know I am God. The Lord of Hosts is with us, the God of Jacob is our refuge.

This, for me, is the key phrase in the psalm: "Be still, and know that I am God." The events that have unfolded make no sense; they can fill us with fear, with anger, with a longing for retribution. And, as we come together in a different world from the one in which we lived last week, in a place where all of these feelings swell up in us, we know that we can and must make choices that will affect our lives as a nation. We have the choice to give in to the same hatred and irrationality that was dealt to us or to hear that still, small voice—"Be still and know that I am God"—before we decide to take any action or make any broad pronouncements.

I have been asked by some of you to talk about the "700 Club" program that aired the day after the attacks. It is a good example of the fact that all faiths, including our own, have hateful adherents. Pat Robertson and Jerry Falwell, the religious right's high bishops of buffoonery, went on the air in front of millions of viewers and laid the blame for the attacks on America squarely on gays, lesbians, and feminists, and the fact that God caused this destruction because this nation tolerates them.

This kind of talk should be a reminder to us that there are millions of devout, loving Muslims who deplore the violence caused by radical fundamentalist terrorists and that we cannot, in any good conscience, allow ourselves to be in the presence of rhetoric that demonizes the Muslim faith without interjecting our full disagreement.

For just as much as one type of fundamentalism allows those of great ignorance to paint the Muslim faith with a broad paintbrush, we have only to look at home and within our own faith to know that demonic forces exist that would distort our gospel of love to perpetrate soulless hate. The Falwells and the Robertsons of this country are nothing more than spiritual terrorists, who this week, in the light of the worst tragedy we have known, hijacked planes of American civility and tolerance and crashed them where flames of hatred would grow.

Such unspeakable hatred exists in every community and in every faith around the world.

But make no mistake. The ground is firm under our feet, a spiritual foundation is still with us, the Lord of Hosts is at our side, and we will not be alone on the journey ahead.

A group of spiritually and psychically wounded individuals, who have lost a parent, a spouse, a friend, or a child, cannot yet return to a time when feelings, conversations, memories, and sometimes even the colors around them seem too vivid in their hurt and anguish. Will these feelings ever stop or, at least, abate, and how long will they be so wounded? I can look into their eyes and see the bewilderment and hurt that demands a rational reason or purpose where none exists.

> Be still, and know that I am God; your path has a purpose, now more than
> ever, even when it shifts, even if the earth should change and the mountains
> fall into the sea, let go and trust in God.

I recall the words of Gandhi: "When every hope is gone, 'when helpers fail and comforts flee,' I experience that help arrives somehow, from I know not where. Being still today in worship and prayer is no superstition; they are acts more real than the acts of eating, drinking, sitting, or walking. It is no exaggeration to say that they, the thoughts of God alone are real, all else is unreal."

There is a hymn that asks: "Oh God, my God, why do you seem so far away?" The question of theodicy, or "where is a loving God when tremendous tragedy befalls," is on many people's minds this week. Many will have their faith shaken and some may lose it. Many young people who are just coming to terms with their beliefs may become angry and distant from God, and we must watch out for them. On the back table today, I have left copies of helpful ideas from our own denomination in finding resources to talk to children about what has happened. I hope every parent will take one and will really consider taking steps to be with their children as they express their feelings. I look at our kids and think that many of them are too young to understand, but then I remember being eight years old, and I can tell you exactly where I was and what I was thinking when I heard that President Kennedy was killed.

I watched an interview about an entire company headquarters that was wiped out, its employees vaporized, and the man at the helm of Cantor-Fitzgerald wept openly on television, wondering how he could continue to tell the families of seven hundred missing employees that they have vanished in the fumes of hatred.

Where is God in this tragedy, that leaves the owner of Cantor-Fitzgerald to suffer while thousands perish, and we are all left to pick up the pieces? "Oh God, my God, my gracious God, why do you seem so far away?"

His remaining employees, many of who have lost their own partners, called him and told him that they have voted to return to work the next day, and America's bond markets reopened. The deep humanity of this man compelled them to have strength and to shoulder the burden of letting this nation and the nations of the world know that we will not be afraid, we will not be destroyed, and we will reemerge, I hope, as better citizens of the world. God is their refuge and their strength. "Be still, and know that I am God."

From partners around the world this nation must relearn about care and compassion, mercy and grace, this time from being on the receiving end of it. The still, small voice that stirs the world has whispered words that have brought about deeds of great compassion and graciousness as we have seen from Great Britain to Iran. Perhaps some of our own acts of arrogance in the world (for we have been an arrogant nation) will now be tempered by these words and deeds of mercy and of love, and we may learn to have humility again.

There is a final question: Where, then, is God? Where is God when terrible tragedies befall us?

Where was God this week? God was not in the cockpit of those four planes. God did not cause this to happen.

In our scripture lesson this morning, we see a glimpse of a Jesus who would leave the ninety-nine sheep behind in order to rescue the one who was lost.

This week, time after time, in the stories of great courage that we have been privileged to hear, there are stories of those who walked into danger in order to try and rescue the lost sheep everywhere:

God in the faces of those of you here and all over this city and country who spent hours in line in order to give blood; one pint of your blood to be there when the one who was lost is found.

God is in the faces of those who searched the hospitals without stopping, in search of that special someone who could not be accounted for.

For all of those who stopped everything they were doing and then moved as if compelled to go down to that site and be on hand to fetch and carry. Or to feed and quench the thirst of the rescue workers that dug through the debris and the book to try and find the lost brothers and sisters, sons and daughters, husbands, wives and partners.

Brett Blair said of this, "That's where God was this week—God was there in the last moments as loved ones used cell phones to say, 'I love you. I am trapped on a plane or trapped on the top floor with no way of escape, I just wanted you to know that I love you.' God was there in the fireman's suit. God stood there behind police badges. God is behind the scalpel and the scrubs. God is near the heart of all, who in the face of this tragedy, love their neighbor and who also still love God. Those whose faith will rise in the ashes of these last few days look to God, not for answers, but because in the end tragedies teach us that we are mortal and fully dependent upon God.[1]

But as mortals, it is only natural for us to ask questions. What should we do? We should mourn.

Yes, we should take time to mourn, but then we must also begin to reflect as we rebuild. We will rebuild our walls as soon as the rubble is cleared. We will rebuild our lives over a longer course after we honor in death all those who have fallen.

We have already begun to rebuild our confidence as a people by showing our solidarity and care. In countless candlelight vigils in countless cities, including one our own church steps, God is with us, our refuge and strength in present time of trouble.

Who is to blame? It is true that America has many things to be ashamed of. Just as do members of every nation and every faith, including the scurrilous televangelist moneychangers of our own.

But, we have done nothing to warrant such atrocities. This is the work of evil as it resides within men, and not of a vengeful God.

Where is God? God is here. Anguish is no stranger to God. Jesus suffered. He died. But he lives within us. Therefore, we have hope in these worst of times.

In every act of kindness, in every outpouring of love and generosity that you have witnessed in story after story on the news, and in the flags, symbols and candles that now line our streets, God is there, and in the catch in your throat and the tears that sometimes just suddenly come when you witness these things, you know and I know that perfect love casts out all fear. And, "therefore, we will not fear, though the earth shall change."

We are many of us of different minds and opinions. We will go through many emotions and feelings here together. This *is* the "beloved community." Treat each other well as you sort out your feelings. Some will want retribution, swift and sure. Others will cry for peace at all costs. Listen to these voices—they are expressing what they need to express, and the feelings are valid simply because you are experiencing them and need to express them.

William Sloane Coffin once said, "Hope, as opposed to cynicism and despair, is the sole precondition for new and better experiences. Realism demands pessimism but hope demands that we take a dim view of the present because we hold a bright view of the future; and hope arouses as nothing else can arouse."[2]

Hope is real. Hope is palpable. All of us together are greater than any one of us singly in lifting up hope for a new day ahead. Today we will walk out of these doors onto the paths our hope will light for us. "I know this path," said Gandhi, "The foundation is strong and firm, it is straight and narrow. I rejoice to walk on it, I weep when I slip. God's word is, 'He who strives never perishes;' I have implicit faith in that promise." We place the first foot forward. "Be still, and know that I am God."

Amen and God bless America.

1. Brett Blair, "A Nation Mourns," from the Christian Globe Network Web site <www.christianglobe.com> resources for September 11.
2. William Sloane Coffin, *Passion for the Possible: A Message to U.S. Churches* (Louisville, Ky.: Westminster/John Knox Press, 1993).

Pray That You May Not Come into the Time of Trial

✿

M. DOUGLAS MEEKS

Scripture: Isaiah 49:8–17; Luke 22:39–46

FORTY-EIGHT HOURS AGO, it was a beautiful fall morning in New York and Washington. The morning habits and rituals of great cities were being followed by their inhabitants. A primary election for mayor had just gotten underway in New York. Then, out of a hellish vacuum of history, came the explosions that have changed history. At first, disbelief had a strangle hold on us. This cannot be happening. As in the moments between sleep and waking, we wanted a bad dream to dissolve into the air. But the unimaginable became real. Within an hour-and-a-half, we seemed to be ensconced, like lower Manhattan, in an ashen shell of horror and grief.

And now we are trying to remember what life was like fifty hours ago and wonder whether we will look back at all our history through billowing smoke and falling debris. The twin towers of world trade and the pentagonal fortress, the symbols of our invincible economic and military power, now reveal themselves as all along vulnerable. We now understand that they stood only because these evil acts were something no human being would do and no human being would be capable of doing. Now we know that these acts can be done by human beings; we know that human beings can cause a sacrifice of burning flesh to the gods of hatred; we know that what we trusted to secure our future, and what we had given an almost divine status to is, after all, subject to history. It's not just that we won't forget 9-11; it was a day that for us split history and catapulted us into terrible uncertainty. It has become one of those moments in our collective life when we can only cry out to God. Even those who consider themselves atheists, when faced with these events, could only mutter, "My God." And for believers, there is no possible response but prayer: "Lord have mercy. Christ have mercy. Lord have mercy." There is no answer for the terror, suffering, and death of so many people. There is no answer for the evil and vanity of the hearts of those who did these deeds. And so we turn to prayer.

But how can we pray? We are able to pray only because we are in the company of Jesus. We pray together with the one whose life began with the slaughter of the innocents; the one who himself experienced the terrorism of the state on the cross, the one who died for a world that seems ruled by violence and hatred, the one who descended into hell and, therefore, can stand with all who suffer from any kind of terrorism. We are able to pray not because we have all the answers—we don't. We are able to pray not because our theology is brimful of a beautiful picture of God that can withstand the human heart's imagination of evil and our own unknowing, stiff-necked service of injustice. No, we pray because the Son of God is suffering in the midst of this tragedy and every human tragedy. We pray because we, too, are in Gethsemane with the one whose own prayer is so anguished that he sweats great drops of blood in uttering, "Not my will but yours be done."

And so we turn to prayer. But like the disciples at the Mount of Olives, our prayer comes with great struggle or does not come at all as we fall into a stupor. And so our Lord commands, "Pray that you may not come into the time of trial." Prayer is the time of greatest temptation.

A. "Pray that you may not come into the time of trial." We will fall into temptation if we do not lift up the suffering and the dead to God in prayer. We are tempted to make ourselves responsible for the explanation of these tragic deaths; we are tempted to think that we can carry the burden of such immense suffering. It is not so. Only the Lord can take the dead. We give him our dead because we have no power over death. In him, who is the resurrection and the life, they will find the power of life against death. We give to the Lord the immeasurable suffering of those who have died and the continuing bitter suffering of their loved ones who are living through their deaths. Only when we give to God the dead and human suffering are we able to continue to suffer with them, and that means to stay in love with them.

B. "Pray that you may not come into the time of trial." A second temptation in prayer is to stay in our own grief. If you are in love with those who are living, grief will be a part of your life, for those you love are subject to death. Only those with the power to suffer will be able to stay in love with the living and the dead. Grief, then, is in fact a sign of life in the human being who grieves. But we are tempted to stay in our grief and thus to fall into a numb and listless death-before-death. To be caught up in grief completely is to live against the reality of the resurrection.

Therefore our prayer must lift up and give up our own grief to the Lord. Grief is not the end and goal of the Christian life. Jesus comes to his disciples and finds them "sleeping because of their grief." He rebukes us disciples when we fall into the slumber of listless resignation. God is not giving up on the world for whose redemption God has suffered so much. Neither may we. We've got work to do—against the forces that would let the world continue its spiral into the vicious circle of violence. Prayer is not only patient waiting on God; it is also patient and chastened action. Prayer means wake up; stand up; get to work.

C. "Pray that you may not come into the time of trial." A third temptation in prayer is to search for false security. Prayer can be uttered to a false god. We might as well confess to God and to each other our anxiety and fear, our crushing loss of a sense of security. Fortress America has been breached. If a flight full of New York to L.A. commuters can be turned into a missile of war, everything is suddenly dangerous, and nothing is completely secure. How are our national security systems supposed to thwart bad intentions if hijackers are now suicidal? How are our lives supposed to be secure if the very wonders of our technology, our vaunted machines of transportation and communication, are turned against us in such a deadly way? How can we remain "first" in the world if the greatest inventions of our minds and products of our industrial prowess no longer set us apart but, rather, are the means of our vulnerability? Suddenly, we are like the other nations.

We will, of course, join our fellow citizens in searching for appropriate security for our people and appropriate justice for the terrorists. But lest we fall into temptation, our prayer must open up a moment in history in which we finally realize that overcoming terrorism does not depend on the increased security of the United States. It depends on the increased security of the global village. If anyone in the world is insecure, we are insecure. Insecurity on which terrorism feeds stems from poverty. Insecurity feeds on newborn babies who live only a few months. Insecurity looms from the arrogance of some nations thinking themselves messianically superior to others.

Will all the world's cities end in a pile of rubbish to be hissed at? Those who cry out to the Lord of Peace will find the city's security and welfare in God's justice and will, therefore, be found among "the builders who outdo the destroyers of the city" (Is. 49:17).

D. "Pray that you may not come into the time of trial." A fourth temptation in prayer is that we would call on God for revenge. Our nation is full of understandable grief and anger. But the talk shows and, tragically, some of our leaders are also full of the call for retaliation. The *lex talionis*, the law of revenge, is the oldest law we human beings know. But since Cain spilled the blood of Abel and the soil cried out in horror, we have known that revenge simply continues the vicious circle of violence. No terrorist can ply his trade without revenge. Terrorists should be brought to justice, but revenge will reward the terrorists' acts with more terror. So in these days, lest we fall into temptation, our prayer should rise to God together with the prayer of our Muslim and Arab neighbors, and, in assurance of the peace that passes understanding, we should pray for our enemies. Thanks be to you, O God, for the merciful presence of Jesus so that we may pray to you in this time of misery.

This is the morning prayer delivered by M. Douglas Meeks at Vanderbilt Divinity School, Wightman Chapel, September 13, 2001. Reprinted by permission from the United Church of Christ EKU Working Group resource, "You Gave the Weary Your Hand" (November 2001).

A Pastoral Prayer for Christmas Eve or Christmas Day, 2001

BRUCE LARSON

O GOD OF JUSTICE, LOVE, AND PEACE, we must confess that our prayer to you this Christmas Day (this Christmas Eve) betrays our trust in you. For our lives are in turmoil; we fear the terror that has been unleashed upon us. Like a caged tiger that we cannot see, our discomfort paces back and forth, back and forth, in the depths of our minds, taunted by the sirens of a fire truck, by the words and images of the latest newscast.

"What's next?" we wonder, "Will we be able to meet the next challenge that is thrust upon us?"

Yet, we remember that Joseph and Mary also faced terror. They, too, were forced to travel through unfamiliar terrain, only to discover no room for them when Mary's time came to deliver the baby. So they had to borrow a stable for the delivery room and had to use a feeding trough for the newborn's crib.

Yes, O God, we know all too well that the pungent squalor of that stable yielded the Savior of the world. But we could never have guessed it, not even in our wildest imaginings, that you, the Creator of the cosmos, would be so born! Likewise, this day (this night) we strive to imagine knowing your peace in our unsettled lives.

Can it be, O God, that the One who had no place at his birth can now have a place in our hearts?

Can it be, O God, that the love this baby would later share with the world can soothe our frazzled nerves right now?

Can it be, O God, that the peace passing all understanding may gently have its way in us and among us this day (this night)?

We pray that this might be so and that you would bring your healing touch to all of us in this time of need and especially to those we mention now: [Pastor or congregants may speak individuals' names]. For those we have spoken aloud and for those we have remembered in silence, we trust you, O God, to lift us from our fear and settle us into your comforting love, so that we may reflect your care for ourselves and for those around us in the coming days.

We know not what the future brings, O God. Even so, we commit it to you, trusting that you will bring to fulfillment your loving will for all of creation. In the name of Jesus,*we pray, Amen.

*alternate ending: who taught his disciples to pray, saying, "Our Father, who . . ."

This prayer was written by Dr. Bruce Larson, minister for campus ministries and students with the Worship and Education Ministry Team of Local Church Ministries: A Covenanted Ministry of the United Church of Christ. The prayer seeks to be sensitive to the tragedy of September 11, 2001, and the desire for peace expressed in "Pronouncement on Affirming the United Church of Christ as a Just Peace Church." For more information about the proclamation, see on-line <www.ucc.org>. Reprinted by permission.

A Litany for Christmas Eve or Christmas Day, 2001

❀

BRUCE LARSON

One: Come, you who labor in faith
　　　without tasting the fruit of your labor,
　　　Look! Your deliverance dawns upon you!

Many: 'God-with-us' is born!
　　　The baby in the manger is our hope.

One: Come, you who tremble in the midst of terror.
　　　Rest from your anxiety!
　　　Sigh with relief!

Many: 'God-with-us' is born!
　　　The baby in the manger is our peace.

One: Come, you who live in loneliness
　　　with no one being near.
　　　You need not be lonely anymore.

Many: 'God-with-us' is born!
　　　The baby in the manger is our love.

One: Come, you who are worn out
　　　by the busy-ness of this season.
　　　Your weariness passes away.

Many: 'God-with-us' is born!
　　　The baby in the manger is our joy.
　　　Alleluia! Christ is here!

This prayer was written by Dr. Bruce Larson, minister for campus ministries and students with the Worship and Education Ministry Team of Local Church Ministries: A Covenanted Ministry of the United Church of Christ. The prayer seeks to be sensitive to the tragedy of September 11, 2001, and the desire for peace expressed in "Pronouncement on Affirming the United Church of Christ as a Just Peace Church." For more information about the proclamation, see on-line <www.ucc.org>. Reprinted by permission.

Bearing Our Grief and Making for Peace

�֎

JUSTICE AND WITNESS MINISTRIES

THE HORRIFIC TERRORIST ATTACKS of Tuesday, September 11, were hate-inspired crimes against all humanity, leaving thousands dead and wounded while millions around the world have been left to grieve under a heavy burden of shock, sorrow, anger, and fear.

The United Church of Christ, like so many other religious traditions, is beginning to learn more fully the direct impact of this tragedy on many of our own faith communities. Already among the confirmed dead are members of our United Church of Christ congregations. We already know that congregations in New York, New Jersey, Connecticut, Massachusetts, Virginia, and the District of Columbia have experienced tremendous sorrow, as multiple families have experienced the death of family members and dear friends.

The United Church of Christ's Justice and Witness Ministries offers our prayers, solidarity, and financial gifts on behalf of those who have been victimized by these murderous deeds of destruction. We, like so many, are filled with an abiding, gnawing grief.

"We are all overwhelmed by the destruction caused by this profound act of hatred," said Bernice Powell Jackson, executive minister of Justice and Witness Ministries. "But we have hope from God to draw upon, the strength of one another, and our own personal and collective stories of overcoming tremendous struggle. We rely on the saving strength of God's grace."

Even in the midst of death and destruction, however, we are already witnessing incredible signs of love, hope, and resurrection. United Church of Christ members and congregations are responding with generous acts of kindness and charity, even while our pastors and lay leaders are helping us to individually name our deep sorrow and collectively share these heavy burdens. This, we must recognize, is part of the heroic work and healing of God.

Still, to be sure, this tragedy is a significant challenge to faith. It raises those timeless questions about the nature of evil and the oftentimes damaging assumptions about God's will in the midst of suffering. Above all, we are invited to hear God's word of hope and allow faith and love to shape our response, even while our tempers may flare with anger and our imaginations may race with images of revenge. More than ever, we are called to reflect on why there is much hatred in the world against the United States and our policies.

At such times, we are reminded of Christ's shocking, yet inspiring, words: "Love your enemies and pray for those who persecute you, so that you may be children of your Creator in heaven" (Mt. 5:44–45). As our nation prepares for war in an effort to confront terrorism, we are challenged by Jesus' call for his followers to be peacemakers. Our own United Church of Christ tradition is filled with a profound history of peaceful resistance, as people of faith have sought to follow in the nonviolent steps of our Lord. As Martin Luther King Jr. said, "Without justice, there is no peace." There are no easy answers, yet the call to faithfulness remains.

Unfortunately, violence has escalated even beyond the horror of that tragic Tuesday. As a nation readies for war, hate crimes against Arab Americans, those perceived to be from the Middle East, and other people of color have risen at staggering rates.

According to the Council on American-Islamic Relations, the FBI and the Justice Department have begun investigating what Arab-American leaders describe as a wave of anti-Muslim violence—from a series of assaults in New York to shots fired at an Irving, Texas, mosque to the attempted burning of the Islamic Idriss Mosque in Seattle.

The Council on American-Islamic Relations reported 210 incidents of violence or threats of violence since the Tuesday-morning attacks on the World Trade Center and the Pentagon.

As you and your congregation wrestle with the events surrounding this national tragedy, Justice and Witness Ministries encourages you:

- To revisit the basic tenets of our own faith and to ask the hard questions about the church's role as an agent of peace and reconciliation. In the United Church of Christ, in light of this tragedy, what does it mean to be a Just Peace Church? We invite and welcome your responses to this difficult question.

- To advocate with government officials for more reasoned political solutions rather than relying solely on military responses.

- To explore the multiple dimensions of violence in our society and to discern ways for your congregation to address those systems that perpetuate violence in your community and the world: poverty and economic inequity, prejudice and racial injustice, stereotyping, scapegoating, and religious persecution. In July, the General Synod called on all settings of the United Church of Christ to join in the National Decade to Overcome Violence.

- To discuss the dangers of fundamentalism in any faith and how it distorts the essential tenets of any religious tradition.

- To reach out in love and friendship to our Muslim brothers and sisters, as well as people of all faith traditions. Only through interfaith understanding and solidarity can true peace be established.

- To be a voice in your community against hate crimes.

- To learn more about Islam and the Middle East so that you might be an enlightened and compassionate voice in an increasing climate of religious hostility and racial prejudice.

- To discuss the differences between patriotism and nationalism and to prayerfully consider how God's love and concern for all people calls us to look beyond national borders in the pursuit of justice and peace.

- To resist any movement to use this tragedy as the mechanism to promote racial hatred or to blame or scapegoat any group of people—or to advance opportunistic political agendas that unnecessarily escalate militarism and violence while ignoring other needs of people in this country and around the world.

From the United Church of Christ Web site <www.ucc.org>, September 2001. Reprinted by permission.

EVERY GOOD PATH

Supporting Faith with Knowledge

~

If you indeed cry out for insight,
and raise your voice for understanding;
if you seek it like silver, and search for it as
for hidden treasures—then you will
understand the fear of the Lord and find
the knowledge of God. . . . Then you will
understand righteousness and justice
and equity, every good path.

—Proverbs 2: 3–5

You must make every effort to support
your faith with goodness, and goodness
with knowledge.

—2 Peter 1:5

~

BEFORE SEPTEMBER 11, 2001, MOST AMERICANS—INCLUDING most faithful Christians—had never heard of the al-Qu'aida Network. They did not recognize the name of Osama bin Laden. They were unaware that nearly six million Muslims—more than four times the membership of the United Church of Christ—were living in towns and cities and even rural areas around the country as peaceful, productive citizens. Before September 11, many Americans—including faithful Christians—had never reflected on the ways in which action, or inaction, in one part of the globe profoundly affects life in other parts. They had not thought about the ways in which the vast gulf between the haves and the have-nots of the world engenders smoldering hatred and violence born of desperation. They knew little or nothing about the twenty-year history of war and famine in a remote mountainous country called Afghanistan and still less about its leaders' alleged connection to international terrorism.

All that changed after September 11.

After September 11, Americans, including faithful Christians, had new eyes and new questions. Together we asked: Who are these people, and why do they hate us so much? How is it that our different cultures shape the ways we interpret one another's actions, even one another's history? What does it mean to be part of an emerging "global village," in which all of us are implicated in a common destiny? And, most importantly, what does our distinctive calling as Christians demand that we now learn about this global village and our neighbors so that we may be responsive to God's desire for a world unshattered by escalating violence and hatred?

The Greater Terror

❀

AUGUSTO N. MICLAT JR.

My one-cent's worth on last Tuesday's carnage . . .

SUDDENLY, EVERYTHING SEEMS SO PUNY.

After the terror in Manhattan and D.C., the larger and day-to-day problems of humanity seem to have been further forgotten.

The entire world continues to be transfixed with the vivid images of planes slamming into skyscrapers; of smoke and dust billowing unceasingly from the rubble of New York's icon, melted to smithereens; of debris cascading like liquid to the ground, flowing into the streets and alleys of downtown Manhattan; of desperate bodies clinging to window sills or plunging to their bloody deaths; of able-bodied rescuers and policemen and survivors drenched in soot, blood, sweat, and tears.

Television and tabloids with these same pictures and stories assault our senses like a tireless Hollywood movie rewind.

Then there are those shrill voices engulfing the air, from righteous rage to self-righteous bigotry. Of the doomsday prophet's "I told you so" to the rabid zealot's "let's bomb the hell out of them." Of the instant analyst's "a catastrophic intelligence failure" to the politician pandering to raw emotions, "he better say his prayers." Reason and calm are altogether drowned by jingoistic and irrational responses, contributed to largely by a skewed media coverage. Indeed, the feelings are real; the anger is fresh; the pain and numbness slice through the marrow of one's soul. The struggle for peace will be more tedious.

The savagery in Manhattan need not be denigrated. It should be condemned with the loudest, unrelenting voice of all civilized peoples. The perpetrators behind this evil deed and their sponsors should be brought to justice as swiftly as possible. Our hearts bleed for the thousands of innocent victims and their kin. Mothers, fathers, children, friends, and neighbors. Unlike combatants, they had no inkling of nor were they prepared for their fiery end when they boarded the ill-fated planes or reported for work on an ordinary, bright ,Tuesday morning at their swank offices in the belly of Manhattan and Washington. Ditto for the firefighters and police who simply responded to secure and rescue lives but ended up adding to the toll instead.

Indeed, nobody will ever feel safe in this world again.

But,

While we grieve, mourn, sympathize, and seethe over Tuesday's carnage, we must remember and address the daily terrors of our lives. And while doing so, perhaps unlock the insanity leading to the devastation in Manhattan, Washington, and Pittsburgh.

For terror is not the sole domain of fanatics and zealots. Terror is not just borne out of loathing and helplessness at the injustices of the mighty against the puny. Terror is not only hatched in the bunkers of dingy hotel rooms and apartments.

Terror is also, if not more so, concocted in brightly lit corporate boardrooms and in the august chambers of powerful governments and military fortresses.

It is this kind of terror that has consigned the bulk of humanity to poverty and destitution, to perpetual debt, and to the ravages of preventable diseases; to the mercy of sanctions and embargoes and the whims of the market and xenophobic policy paradigms.

It is the kind of terror that doesn't have cameras to document the anguish of our mothers, fathers, children, and neighbors after bombs released from high-flying planes flatten our communities and souls, when tanks roll into our farms, when our child dies for lack of rudimentary medication or basic services, when our land or job is taken away from us.

It is the kind of terror in the eyes of the mother cradling her bloodied son in the West Bank; of a frail father muttering a prayer for his wilting daughter in a hospital in Baghdad, of a Sudanese fleeing a bomb-ravaged pharmaceutical factory. It is the terror of refugees turned away on the high seas off Australia or living in squalor in camps in the fringes of Thailand, West Timor, or Mindanao; of impaled Serbs, Bosnians, and Acehnese; of imprisoned and tortured Burmese and Tamils; of hungry Bangladeshis and Angolans; of sacked Filipino and Colombian workers—the terror almost everybody else stares down daily in their lives outside of the United States of America.

It is also the terror of the hungry black bears foraging in downtown Albuquerque because the forests are sick; of frightened deer of the wounded Amazon jungle; of scarred whales in the Pacific, harpooned to whet exotic appetites; of eagles caged so they can breed.

It is the terror that has accompanied us in our lifetimes and that has been shunted aside by the likes of CNN because it is not news enough nor cushy enough for the American way of life.

It is the terror of a sick world, unhinged from its balance because of the wanton craving for profits and power. And it is the terror likewise unhitched from its victims for redress.

While we try to make sense out of Tuesday's atrocity, as we come to grips with the loss and emptiness that we collectively share, as others rant for blood and vengeance, as politicians, generals, and corporations surf on this wave of outrage to push their cold and profitable agendas, it is perhaps best to pay heed to Kofi Anan's call for cool and reasonable responses to this calamity. Not doing so will only rouse the voracious lust of those silent, subtle, cunning terrorists ensconced in the corridors of the poor who will in no time push this world to the brink of colossal disaster.

And the greater terror is not being able to recognize this tragedy.

Gus Miclat is the executive director of Initiatives for International Dialogue, Davao City, Philippines.

This was a general e-mail sent to the United Church of Christ on September 16, 2001. Reprinted by permission.

Who Are These People, and Why Do They Hate Us So Much?

❀

DALE BISHOP

MY SON IS SPENDING the next three months in Spain working on an organic farm. En route to Spain from a beleaguered New York City that has been his home for all of his eighteen years, Andrew sent me an e-mail: "Dad, please don't visit any predominantly Islamic country." This from a young man whose father has probably averaged at least three visits per year to "predominantly Islamic countries" for the last twenty years.

In the wake of the murderous attacks on the World Trade Center and the Pentagon, attacks presumably carried out by Muslims who claim their religion as their motivation, all of the old suspicions about and fears of Islam have reemerged, but now with a special urgency.

Some theorists have evoked the dichotomy of Islam versus the West. They argue that the terrorists and, by extension, all Muslims carry an undying enmity for all things western, including democratic institutions, "modernity," and human rights. While Iran's President Mohammad Khatami has called for a "dialogue of civilizations," talk-show experts refer blithely to the "war of civilizations."

People who think that I know something about these things have been asking me what boils down to the same question, "Who are these people, and why do they hate us so much?"

Let me begin by stating the obvious, but maybe not so obvious, given the kinds of questions people are asking. Muslims, followers of Islam, are human beings. Some are very religious, and some are more indifferent to their inherited religious tradition. To refer to someone as a Muslim tells us no more and no less than referring to someone as a Christian. To find out "who people are," we need to look at each person as a unique individual, shaped in large part by that person's context and history; someone who, to a greater or lesser extent, is trying to make sense of that context and history in the light of religious belief.

Christians are close to Muslims, as they are to Jews, in our common monotheism. We share a belief in one sovereign God, even though our different linguistic traditions give that God different names in different places. The Arabic word for God, Allah, is the word also used by Arab Christians. Most Muslims will be offended by the formulation, "your God," or "the God of Islam," because they believe that this one God is the source of our common revelation in the Abrahamic tradition. They do believe that the scriptures of Christians and Jews are less complete and accurate because they were written down well after the actual revelation took place; for Muslims, the Quran, the record of God's revelation through the Prophet Muhammad, is complete and without flaw. But, because there is one God, there is one revelation of God's will brought to humanity by a series of prophets, including the Hebrew prophets and Jesus, and culminating with Muhammad.

If we are so close, I am sometimes asked, why do we seem so different? Muslims are often seen as angry and vengeful, while Christians speak the language of love. Or so it seems.

Muslims, for example, believe in the duty, when called on, to participate in *jihad*, which is often translated as "holy war." The Taliban of Afghanistan, we are told, have declared a *jihad* against the United States. *Jihad*, however is a far more complex concept than the simplistic interpretation of "holy war" would suggest. In fact, *jihad*, whose basic meaning is "struggle," can be and has often been applied to the spiritual struggle to be faithful and to discern the will of God. This personal quest is referred to as "the greater *jihad*."

The kind of *jihad* we hear about, the one that has to do with struggling with the enemies of the faith, is probably better translated to Christian audiences as "the just war." As in the Christian "just war" tradition, there are, in fact, criteria that are to be met before a *jihad* may be authorized, and once it has been authorized, there are rules of conduct of war that must be adhered to. The enemy must pose a threat to the community; the response to that threat must be proportional; attacks on civilians are forbidden, especially on women, children, and the elderly; buildings are not to be destroyed; sneak attacks are forbidden.

Are these criteria consistently applied? No more than every "just war" has been proportional or without civilian victims. What Christian "just war" theories have in common with *jihad* is the belief that God approves certain kinds of warfare.

During the period leading up to the Gulf War, President Bush the elder simultaneously declared that, "God is on our side," while Saddam Hussein was calling for a *jihad* against America. Without intending disrespect to our former president, neither he nor Saddam really were authorized within their own religious traditions to make such declarations about the will of God. President Bush and his Iraqi counterpart were seeking religious justification for political decisions.

Our current President Bush also has invoked God in his comments about the response to the recent terrorist attacks, and even, in an early and really ill-advised comment, referred to our effort as a "crusade." Fortunately, that characterization was subsequently withdrawn. It is, after all, difficult to imagine enlisting the help of Islamic countries in something called a "crusade." All this is to say that Christians and Muslims alike, perhaps because we regard God as important in our lives, tend to want to invoke divine approval for our undertakings, even if those undertakings run contrary to the best of our traditions.

Which brings us back to the second part of that question, "Why do they hate us so much?" Well, actually, most don't. There are different levels of feeling toward the United States and, by extension, the Christian West, depending pretty much on what people's experiences of us have been.

Many Muslims from abroad, like other immigrants, have sought to create new lives here, to live in peace and prosperity with their neighbors. They have grieved over the recent events with the same intensity of feeling that the rest of us have felt. How they are treated in the wake of the attacks will affect not only their perception of American society, but also the perceptions of friends and families in their countries of origin.

Others have felt themselves to be victimized by American policy, particularly the Palestinians and the Iraqis, but their plight is felt throughout the Islamic world, again, with varying levels of intensity.

Earlier, in my career as Middle East area executive with the United Church Board for World Ministries, I exchanged correspondence with a member of the United Church of Christ who worked with the Defense Intelligence Agency. He had taken issue with something I had written, and, in the course of our exchange of letters, he wrote that, in the long run, the Arabs will have no alternative but to ally themselves with the United States. The Soviet Union was already in decline, in part because of their ill-fated venture in Afghanistan, and there were simply no other options left. It is precisely when people feel that they have no real options that they do extreme things.

Almost everyone I met in the Middle East over the years made the distinction between me as an individual American and the policies and behavior of my government. I think this is why, aside from some isolated incidents among the Palestinians, there was an overwhelming sympathy for the losses sustained by American families in the attacks on New York and Washington.

That doesn't mean that criticism of the United States will abate in the aftermath of these events, but it represents a basic belief that innocents should not suffer because their government makes bad decisions.

Clearly, for some, however, a line has been crossed, and a whole society is regarded as fair game. Our ability to distinguish between these relatively few extremists and our potential friends in the Middle East will determine whether al-Qu'aida is the wave of the future, or a passing, if horribly destructive, phenomenon. An American response that extends the circle of victimization is, most likely, the terrorists' real goal. One can only hope that our government will not follow the script that extremists have written for us.

How we define our interests, to put it bluntly, must stand the test of our faith. A Muslim critique, certainly not the only one, of "western Christian society," is that we no longer regard faith to be important enough to have an impact on how we behave as individuals or as a society. The crisis facing us in the wake of these awful events is, I believe, not a crisis of military capability or of financial resilience; it is one of faith.

Do we believe that our faith provides answers as to how we are to conduct ourselves in the world? Or is our faith a privatized and part-time matter? If we believe the former, we will need to come to terms critically not only with how we respond to these current outrages, but also with how we respond to a world in which such desperate disparity exists between those who have and those who have not; between those who exercise power and those who are on its receiving end.

This isn't a matter of politics, although it has political consequences. It really is a matter of faith.

Dale Bishop is executive minister of the United Church of Christ's Wider Church Ministries and a member of the Collegium of Officers. He was the Middle East area executive for the United Church of Christ for twenty-two years. For three of those years, he also performed the same role for the National Council of Churches.

From *United Church News* (October 2001). Reprinted by permission.

A World Out of Touch with Itself

Where the Violence Comes From

❈

MICHAEL LERNER

THERE IS NEVER ANY JUSTIFICATION for acts of terror against innocent civilians—it is the quintessential act of dehumanization and not recognizing the sanctity of others and a visible symbol of a world increasingly irrational and out of control.

It's understandable why many of us, after grieving and consoling the mourners, will feel anger. Demagogues will try to direct that anger at various "target groups" (Muslims are in particular danger, though Yassir Arafat and other Islamic leaders have unequivocally denounced these terrorist acts.) The militarists will use this as a moment to call for increased defense spending at the expense of the needy. Right-wingers may even seek to limit civil liberties, end restraints on spying, and move us toward a militarized society. President Bush will feel pressure to look "decisive" and take "strong" action—phrases that can be manipulated toward irrational responses to an irrational attack.

To counter that potential manipulation of our fear and anger for narrow political ends, a well-meaning media will instead try to narrow our focus solely on the task of finding and punishing the perpetrators. These people, of course, should be caught and punished.

But in some ways this exclusive focus allows us to avoid dealing with the underlying issues. When violence becomes so prevalent throughout the planet, it's too easy to simply talk of "deranged minds." We need to ask ourselves, "What is it in the way that we are living, organizing our societies, and treating each other that makes violence seem plausible to so many people?"

We in the spiritual world will see this as a growing global incapacity to recognize the spirit of God in each other—what we call the sanctity of each human being. But even if you reject religious language, you can see that the willingness of people to hurt each other to advance their own interests has become a global problem, and it's only the dramatic level of this particular attack that distinguishes it from the violence and insensitivity to each other that is part of our daily lives.

We may tell ourselves that the current violence has "nothing to do" with the way that we've learned to close our ears when told that one out of every three people on this planet does not have enough food and that one billion are literally starving. We may reassure ourselves that the hoarding of the world's resources by the richest society in world history and our frantic attempts to accelerate globalization with its attendant inequalities of wealth has nothing to do with the resentment that others feel toward us. We may tell ourselves that the suffering of refugees and the oppressed has nothing to do with us—that that's a different story that is going on somewhere else. But we live in one world, increasingly interconnected with everyone, and the forces that lead people to feel outrage, anger and desperation eventually impact on our own daily lives.

The same sense of disconnection to the plight of others operates in the minds of many of these terrorists. Raise children in circumstances where no one is there to take care of them or where they must live by begging or selling their bodies in prostitution, put them in refugee camps and tell them that that they have "no right of return" to their homes, treat them as though they are less valuable and deserving of respect because they are part of some despised national or ethnic group, surround them with a media that extols the rich and makes everyone who is not economically successful and physically trim and conventionally "beautiful" feel bad about themselves, offer them jobs whose sole goal is to enrich the "bottom line" of someone else, and teach them that "looking out for number one" is the only thing anyone "really" cares about and that anyone who believes in love and social justice are merely naive idealists who are destined to always remain powerless, and you will produce a world-wide population of people feeling depressed, angry, and, in various ways, dysfunctional.

Luckily most people don't act out in violent ways—they tend to act out more against themselves, drowning themselves in alcohol or drugs or personal despair. Others turn toward fundamentalist religions or ultra-nationalist extremism. Still others find themselves acting out against people they love, acting angry or hurtful toward children or relationship partners.

Most Americans will feel puzzled by any reference to this "larger picture." It seems baffling to imagine that somehow we are part of a world system that is slowly destroying the life-support system of the planet and quickly transferring the wealth of the world into our own pockets.

We don't feel personally responsible when an American corporation runs a sweatshop in the Philippines or crushes efforts of workers to organize in Singapore. We don't see ourselves implicated when the U.S. refuses to consider the plight of Palestinian refugees or uses the excuse of fighting drugs to support repression in Colombia or other parts of Central America. We don't even see the symbolism when terrorists attack America's military center and our trade center—we talk of them as buildings, though others see them as centers of the forces that are causing the world so much pain.

We have narrowed our own attention to "getting through" or "doing well" in our own personal lives, and who has time to focus on all the rest of this? Most of us are leading perfectly reasonable lives within the options that we have available to us—so why should others be angry at us, much less strike out against us? And the truth is, our anger is also understandable: The striking out by others in acts of terror against us is just as irrational as the world system it seeks to confront.

When people have learned to treat each other as means to our own ends and to not feel the pain of those who are suffering, they end up creating a world in which these kinds of terrible acts of violence become more common. And as we've learned from the current phase of the Israel–Palestinian struggle, responding to terror with more violence rather than asking ourselves what we could do to change the conditions that generated it in the first place will only ensure more violence in the future.

This is a world out of touch with itself, filled with people who have forgotten how to recognize and respond to the sacred in each other, because we are so used to looking at others from the standpoint of what they can do for us, how we can use them toward our own ends. We should pray for the victims and the families of those who have been hurt or murdered in these crazy acts. We should also pray that America does not return to "business as usual" but rather turns to a period of reflection, coming back into touch with our common humanity, asking ourselves how our institutions can best embody our highest values. We may need a global day of atonement and repentance dedicated to finding a way to turn the direction of our society at every level, a return to the notion that every human life is sacred, that "the bottom line" should be the creation of a world of love and caring, and that the best way to prevent these kinds of acts is not to turn ourselves into a police state but turn ourselves into a society in which social justice, love, and compassion are so prevalent that violence becomes only a distant memory.

Rabbi Michael Lerner is editor of TIKKUN *Magazine and rabbi of Beyt Tikkun Synagogue in San Francisco. He is the author of* Spirit Matters: Global Healing and the Wisdom of the Soul *and, most recently (September 2001), editor of* Best Contemporary Jewish Writing.

Reprinted by permission of *TIKKUN: A Bimonthly Jewish Critique of Politics, Culture, and Society* <www.tikkun.org> (September 12, 2001).

After Terror's Shock

❀

Max L. Stackhouse

THE MANY THINGS that pastors had done as the Untied States lived through the shock of September 11 proved to be quite marvelous. People turned to the church for comfort, with grief, and in dismay at the unexpected, powerful presence of evil. The attack on innocent people, as well as on the economic and political institutions of this land, made many aware of the fact that, while many areas of our social life are not at all beyond prophetic criticism, they are also partially rooted in principles and purposes that have dimensions of moral validity and are also, often in hidden, indirect, and forgotten ways, rooted in the unintended and substantially benevolent effects of the Christian heritage. Many pastors rediscovered loyalties that are not, in fact, contrary to faith.

Moreover, in the performance of their duties, brought to high alert by these events and by the renewed awareness of subtle inter-weavings of Christ with culture, they found words of hope in the face of dismay, conveyed the awareness of presence in the face of loss, revitalized the sense of closeness to the divine channels of meaning in the face of absurdity, and pointed to the rock on which to stand as great artifacts of civilization collapsed into the rubble of Ground Zero. They rightly honored, as they buried and mourned, those called to vocations of service, those whom we often simply presume—the police, the firefighters, the postal workers, the cooks and waiters, the managers of retirement funds—and ministered to their surviving relatives and friends. Many found on a public, macro scale what is most often experienced only in highly personal, micro situations: the people, the nation; sometimes the very people, the very nation, that little attend to what clergy stand for and offer weekly or needed what pastors had to offer. People remembered what they often neglect: Meaning depends on what pastors are called to represent.

Is it not so that many pastors preconsciously renewed their ordination vows and rediscovered the convictions that took them into ministry? It was a great, an unwanted, unexpected revival!

But we now also have another task, one for which we are less prepared. It appears that behind these acts was not only a critique of the economic and political policies of the United States, some of which have been disruptive of cultural values that others hold dear and deserve prophetic judgment, but an interpretation of a religious vision that both overlaps with and differs from our own. In spite of the fact that we live in a global era where faiths do and must encounter each other, most Christian pastors are not prepared to fairly interpret or to critically assess other religions, perhaps most especially Islam, besides Judaism, the other great monotheistic, revelational, and universal faith.

We have been largely disarmed from this now-needed ministry by three developments. One is a widespread form of liberal theology that views all faiths as equally valid and as simply different responses to the divine reality in different cultures. Any judgments would, in this view, be simply the imposition of our cultural perceptions on someone else's A second is the resurgence of dogmatic theology in the last century. It focuses its attention on the internal narratives and doctrines of our own tradition and is contemptuous of all religions. Its capacity to interpret and assess non-Christian faiths has yet to be established. Third, Liberation Theology gives priority to views from the marginalized contexts of the world, especially as they challenge any Euro-American hegemonies: political, economic, cultural, or theological. Whether this mode of reflection can fairly critique any revolutionary praxis that confronts the West is still to be seen.

The fact of a globalized world, which is now confirmed by networks of global terror that compromise the sovereignty of all nations, urgently demands forms of theological competence that can both appreciate the contributions of the world's cultures and religions and critically assess those which, should they become more dominant, would extend the horrors of social destruction.

We may be relatively prepared to offer a mostly accurate portrait and a nuanced critical assessment of Nazi paganism, of Communist secularism, and of New-Age spirituality. Moreover, we may have a profound sense of the intimate, troubled relationship of Judaism and Christianity. But we have not attended to the claims of Islam. How shall we deal with the claims that the revelations to Mohammed, in one sense, supercede the revelations to Moses and in Jesus and, in another sense, restore the more primal relationship of God to humanity? And how shall we deal with a theology of history that understands the human drama as a prescripted story that will ultimately and inevitably lead to the obedience of the whole world to Allah, a history that has been frustrated by the refusal of Jews and Christians (and Buddhists and Hindus) to recognize this truth, a history that, because it has resisted the divine script, may be actualized by violence?

Because of our awareness of the need to confess our sins for evils perpetrated by Christians from the Crusades and witch trials to the Holocaust, we may have abdicated the duty to assess faiths beyond our own. Not only must we face the question of whether we can tell the difference between true and false revelations and give an account of the faith that is within us, we have neglected the contributions of Christianity to justice, democracy, and human rights. No one wants a new Crusade, and we must make clear that the critique of a religion does not entail discrimination against believers in faiths not our own, but we should at least be as critical of fundamentalism in non-Christian garb as we are of fundamentalism within our midst.

With the care of prophetic rigor, pastoral sensibility, and political discernment, we must assume again, in new ways, the offices of Christ—prophet, priest, and king—and guide our congregations and our society to a new kind of non-imperial, culturally pluralistic, world-wide responsibility for the sake of a Godly just peace in an inevitably emerging global society.

Max Stackhouse is the Stephen Colwell Professor of Christian Ethics, Princeton Theological Seminary, Princeton, New Jersey.

Reprinted by permission. From the United Church of Christ EKU Working Group resource, "You Gave the Weary Your Hand" (November 2001), revised from an original e-mail sent to Confessing Christ mailing list.

Make the Afghans Suffer? They're Already Suffering

❀

TAMIM ANSARY

SEPTEMBER 14, 2001—I've been hearing a lot of talk about "bombing Afghanistan back to the Stone Age." Ronn Owens, on San Francisco's KGO Talk Radio, conceded today that this would mean killing innocent people, people who had nothing to do with this atrocity, but, "we're at war, we have to accept collateral damage. What else can we do?" Minutes later I heard some TV pundit discussing whether we "have the belly to do what must be done."

And I thought about the issues being raised especially hard because I am from Afghanistan, and even though I've lived in the United States for thirty-five years, I've never lost track of what's going on there. So I want to tell anyone who will listen how it all looks from where I'm standing.

I speak as one who hates the Taliban and Osama bin Laden. There is no doubt in my mind that these people were responsible for the atrocity in New York. I agree that something must be done about those monsters.

But the Taliban and bin Laden are not Afghanistan. They're not even the government of Afghanistan. The Taliban are a cult of ignorant psychotics who took over Afghanistan in 1997. Bin Laden is a political criminal with a plan. When you think Taliban, think Nazis. When you think bin Laden, think Hitler. And when you think "the people of Afghanistan," think "the Jews in the concentration camps."

It's not only that the Afghan people had nothing to do with this atrocity. They were the first victims of the perpetrators. They would exult if someone would come in there, take out the Taliban, and clear out the rats' nest of international thugs holed up in their country.

Some say, why don't the Afghans rise up and overthrow the Taliban? The answer is, they're starved, exhausted, hurt, incapacitated, suffering. A few years ago, the United Nations estimated that there are 500,000 disabled orphans in Afghanistan—a country with no economy, no food. There are millions of widows. And the Taliban has been burying these widows alive in mass graves. The soil is littered with land mines, the farms were all destroyed by the Soviets. These are a few of the reasons why the Afghan people have not overthrown the Taliban.

We come now to the question of bombing Afghanistan back to the Stone Age. Trouble is, that's been done. The Soviets took care of it already. Make the Afghans suffer? They're already suffering. Level their houses? Done. Turn their schools into piles of rubble? Done. Eradicate their hospitals? Done. Destroy their infrastructure? Cut them off from medicine and healthcare? Too late, someone already did all that. New bombs would only stir the rubble of earlier bombs. Would they at least get the Taliban? Not likely. In today's Afghanistan, only the Taliban eat, only they have the means to move around. They'd slip away and hide.

Maybe the bombs would get some of those disabled orphans; they don't move too fast—they don't even have wheelchairs. But flying over Kabul and dropping bombs wouldn't really be a strike against the criminals who did this horrific thing. Actually, it would only be making common cause with the Taliban—by raping once again the people they've been raping all this time.

So what else is there? What can be done, then? Let me now speak with true fear and trembling. The only way to get bin Laden is to go in there with ground troops. When people speak of "having the belly to do what needs to be done," they're thinking in terms of having the belly to kill as many as needed. Having the belly to overcome any moral qualms about killing innocent people. Let's pull our heads out of the sand. What's actually on the table is Americans dying.

And not just because some Americans would die fighting their way through Afghanistan to bin Laden's hideout. It's much bigger than that, folks. Because to get any troops to Afghanistan, we'd have to go through Pakistan. Would they let us? Not likely. The conquest of Pakistan would have to be first. Will other Muslim nations just stand by? You see where I'm going. We're flirting with a world war between Islam and the West.

And guess what: That's bin Laden's program. That's exactly what he wants. That's why he did this. Read his speeches and statements. It's all right there. He really believes Islam would beat the West. It might seem ridiculous, but he figures if he can polarize the world into Islam and the West, he's got a billion soldiers. If the West wreaks a holocaust in those lands, that's a billion people with nothing left to lose; that's even better from bin Laden's point of view. He's probably wrong—in the end the West would win, whatever that would mean—but the war would last for years and millions would die, not just theirs but ours.

Who has the belly for that? Bin Laden does. Anyone else?

Tamim Ansary is a writer in San Francisco and the son of a former Afghani politician.

From *United Church News* (October 2001). Used by permission.

Reflecting on the Twin Towers from a Human Rights Perspective

❋

Abraham Magendzo Kolstrein

THE TWENTIETH CENTURY, only recently left behind, was forever marked by the Holocaust. It has been maintained, rightly so, that the human story came apart: We could no longer think as we thought before, we could no longer be as we were before, we could no longer live as we lived before, *we could no longer educate as we educated before*. Auschwitz shattered the twentieth century and forced us to rethink everything; it forced us to confront the reality that human beings were capable of absolute cruelty, of wiping out humanity through infinite inhumanity.

Once the war was over, however, we were able to move forward. With the realization that the unthinkable was, in fact, possible, the community of nations drew up a code of ethics so it would never happen again: The Universal Declaration of Human Rights.

But the unthinkable has been possible time and time again. This time, there are no words.

The twenty-first century will be forever marked by the fall of the Twin Towers and with them the lives of so many, their biographies interrupted, their faces wiped away in a moment of inhumanity, recoverable only in memory.

The story of the twenty-first century, begun with such hope after leaving behind the Holocaust century, has come undone. We can no longer think as we thought, no longer be as we were, no longer live as we lived, *no longer educate as we educated*. The Twin Towers tear us away from the hopeful beginning of this century and out of necessity, everything must be rethought.

I am filled with the fear that, instead of taking a step forward as we did after the Holocaust, we will take a step backward, back into the darkest periods of our history; that we will bring forth the most extreme of fanaticisms, the most chilling of discriminations, the most terrifying of intolerances; that we will build walls and divisions to separate ourselves from one another; that we will reinforce distrust, suspicion, and fear; that we each will look around and begin believing, "those who are not with me, do not think like me, do not feel like me, are against me. They are suspicious, abnormal, strange, dangerous beings." In this scenario, the step back would be a return to the belief that, in the interest of "true humanity," the world has to be cleansed of "pseudo-humanity."

And, if so, we will have then called into question the universal code of ethics we gave ourselves and fully entered the law of the jungle, where the means justify the end, where all humanity is suspended.

Caution: I am not saying that the ghastly crimes should be unpunished. No morally competent individual could justify the evil we have experienced. As Agnes Heller says, "Atrocious crimes which should be punished in order for the spirit of historical justice to prevail are those which are manifestations of evil."

But we need to take an extra precaution: While intending to bring about historical justice, we could also bring down the ethical architecture that humanity has worked so hard to build. I ask myself: Is it possible that we might abolish individuals' human rights for the purpose of bringing about historical justice? Are the right to life, the right not to be subjected to torture or to cruel, inhuman, or degrading treatment or punishment still in force? Are we on the brink, perhaps, of doing away with the right to due process, where one is presumed innocent until proven guilty? Might we perhaps, suppress the last article of the Declaration that states: *Nothing in this Declaration may be interpreted as implying for any State, group, or person any right to engage in any activity or to perform any act aimed at the destruction any of the rights and freedoms set forth herein.*

The perpetrators violated these rights and many more. Morally we should not, and cannot, follow in their footsteps.

Japan Reflections

✥

BARBARA BROWN ZIKMUND

OCTOBER 17, 2001

A FEW DAYS AGO in our apartment building, a Japanese man, whom I do not know but who lives in the building, did something I will never forget. As we stood in the lobby waiting for the elevator, we nodded and slightly bowed to each other, as we always do. We mumbled "*Konichi wa*," which means "Hello." However, once we were in the elevator and headed up, he turned to me and said in very carefully chosen words, "So sorry, so sorry." I must have looked a bit puzzled, because I did not think that he had done anything that he needed to apologize for. Then he said, "Sorry, New York, Washington." "Sorry, New York, Washington," shaking his head sadly. I managed to say thank you in Japanese, and then the elevator door opened and he was gone. As I went on to my floor I felt an incredible sense of gratitude and solidarity. He wanted me to know that he cared. It meant a lot. I find myself thinking that, beyond language and culture, decent people all over the world have been profoundly affected by what happened on September 11. Suddenly, we are all neighbors in a new way.

In the first session of my American Thought class, I asked the students to write down three important words describing American thought and values. I told the class that sometimes it is easier to understand another culture when you can contrast it with your own culture. Therefore, I also asked them to write down three important words describing Japanese thought and values. The results are fascinating. Some words were predictable and appeared repeatedly (frequency in parentheses). Others, however, were subtler. I pass along the two lists because I think that they provide an interesting summary of some of the important differences between the United States and Japan.

When asked to describe America, students wrote: freedom (8), democracy (7), individualism (5), liberty (4), equality (3), multicultural, responsibility, strength, optimism, justice, self-reliance, republicanism, hegemony, rationalism, dream, kind, progressive, capitalism, liberalism, tolerant, intolerant, and hamburger.

Then they wrote rather different words to describe Japan: harmony (4), modesty (3), zen (2), cooperation, patience, manners, diligence, homogeneous, samurai spirit, conservative, capitalism, specialization, kind, peace, humbleness, obedience, emotional, totalitarianism, closed society, diversity, equality, spiritual, courtesy, secret, mysterious, group oriented, outside and inside, mutual dependence, average, common, ambiguous, and tea.

As I read the words and compiled the lists, I found myself thinking, "So here I am—living between hamburger and tea, among a people who value harmony, modesty, zen, cooperation, patience, and manners." Japan is a very different culture. Only three words, "capitalism," "equality," and "kind" appeared on both lists. I know that this little exercise has no validity as a poll, yet when I read these two lists of words, they ring true. My Japanese students are proud that they are modest and patient and kind. They want to be mysterious and ambiguous, especially to their "American sensei" (teacher). They respect American values of freedom, democracy, individualism, and liberty from a distance, but they are not "at home" with those ideas. They feel a kinship with the U.S. and its capitalistic way of life (which they embrace, too), but they remain more ambiguous about their affluence.

During the first two weeks of class, I have had many conversations about September 11. One of the more interesting conversations has revolved around the way that the American media has compared the "terrorists" with Japanese "kamikazi pilots" in World War II. Several students said that when they first heard this comparison, they were offended. It seemed to cheapen the sacrifice of Japanese soldiers who gave their lives in the war. Yet, as we talked about the motivations of the terrorists and the motivations of the Japanese pilots, they began to see similarities. At first, the students talked about the terrible "accidents" in New York and Washington. I told them that I did not think that they should call what happened "accidents." Soon one woman commented, "I see, the terrorists, except for the crash in Pennsylvania, did not have an accident. They did exactly what they planned to do. They were not crazy people out of control, they were committed believers giving their lives for something bigger." In that sense, she concluded, they were just like the Japanese pilots in the 1940s. They died, too, because they believed that their death would make a better world. They gave their lives for a cause in which they believed.

This is very disturbing to some of the students. They are not religious in any way, and they find it hard to accept the validity of ANY strongly held beliefs. One student stated that the commitment of Mother Theresa to save the poor in India was no different from the commitment of Osama bin Laden to destroy America. She was afraid of both, because she thinks that strongly held beliefs are very dangerous.

In class, we have talked about motivations. What are people willing to die for? In the American Revolution, Patrick Henry thundered, "Give me liberty, or give me death!" My Japanese students are not sure that it is ever good to be willing to die for something. They think that such commitment is sick or even dangerous. They understand that some people hate the United States. But they have a hard time realizing that many of the terrorists behind the events in New York and Washington probably hate Japan for the very same reasons that they hate the United States. Japan and the United States are both affluent and secular cultures. The Japanese still tend to think that the current global unrest and clash of ideologies is "America's problem."

In my American Thought class this week, we discussed the concept of "equality." This is a concept that is key to understanding American thought. I noted that the word "equality" was one of the few words that had appeared on both lists when I asked the students to put down three words describing American and Japanese culture on the first day of class.

So I asked, "How do the Japanese understand equality?" "Is the Japanese understanding of equality different from what Americans think, and if so, how?" Their response was interesting. One student said, "The Japanese are more concerned about 'the equality of results.' Children are taught to be sensitive to the feelings of others and never to emphasize differences. Japanese manners seek to ensure that no one feels uncomfortable—that all people feel equal—even when there are huge discrepancies between people based on economics or education. Japanese language patterns minimize the power or status of the speaker and always pay deference to others. If I speak about my mother, I use less pretentious words than if I speak about your mother. It is assumed that I have a strong attachment and appreciation for my mother, but I should not show that. Rather, I must go out of my way to compensate linguistically when I speak about your mother in order to give her honor and status equal to my mother. The 'equality of results' is maintained because people take extra care not to emphasize differences or to claim too much status or power for themselves and their families."

When Americans speak and write about "equality," we are not so much concerned about results as about beginnings. Americans believe that everyone should start with an equal chance, an equal opportunity to compete and to win. Americans think that people from different families, economic standing, educational background, and so forth, ought to be equal under the law, ought to have equal opportunity. Indeed, our whole history has been the gradual expansion of equality as "a level place where everyone can begin without disadvantage, or special advantage."

Obviously, Americans know that there are great inequalities in the world. They know that some people will be rich, some will be educated, some will have political power, while at the same time others will be poor, illiterate, and powerless. But the American system tries to guarantee that everyone can begin in the same place. Justice prevails when people have equal rights, not equal results. Fascinating.

Is there a way to blend these two perspectives? Can we create a world where equality of beginnings and an equality of results are valued equally? These are some of the questions we might all want to ponder.

Barbara Brown Zikmund teaches at the Graduate School of American Studies, Doshisha University, Kyoto, Japan, and was formerly president of Hartford Seminary.

Reflections on Japan, October, 17, 2001. Reprinted by permission.

FAITH WORKS

Responding to Disaster with Action

~

What good is it, my brothers and sisters,
if you say you have faith but do not have works? . . .
If a brother or sister is naked or lacks daily food,
and one of you says to them, "Go in peace; keep
warm and eat your fill," and yet you do not supply
their bodily needs, what is the good of that?
So faith by itself, if it has no works, is dead."

—Romans 12:18

~

INDELIBLE IMAGES IN THE AFTERMATH OF TRAGEDY: FIREFIGHTERS, grimy and battered, emerging from the rubble; rescue workers, their faces covered by gas masks and their bodies shrouded in smoke; people of all ages queued up in block-long lines to give blood; roadside shrines, commemorating the lost or missing with mementos and pictures. September 11, 2001, highlighted the mundane heroism of people whose daily work we typically take for granted. For a time, their outrageous selflessness even overwhelmed Manhattan's legendary cynicism.

Most members of the United Church of Christ could not participate directly in helping relief and rescue efforts in either New York or Washington. But, in unprecedented numbers, they went to work in Cleveland and in their own communities. Many came together to pray in special services. "Hope from the Rubble," an appeal for funds to aid victims and survivors, was initiated within a week of the tragedy and administered by Wider Church Ministries. United Church of Christ pastor Robin Meyers, who experienced and ministered through the Oklahoma City bombing tragedy, met with clergy in the middle-Atlantic region to share his knowledge and help pastors cope with the disaster. Specialists in crisis counseling focused on providing long-term and immediate services through an ecumenical "spiritual and emotional care-call center." And throughout the United Church of Christ, local churches and leaders called for members to take personal action against hate crimes and the scapegoating of Muslims, Middle Easterners, and others.

"To Believe Is to Care, to Care Is to Do," reads the familiar bumper sticker first printed by the Maine Conference of the United Church of Christ. For many Americans, outreach in the wake of September 11 was a healthy form of self-care, a way to keep feelings of impotence and outrage at bay. For Christians, it was and is much more: the gospel imperative to make outwardly manifest the hope that—even in the midst of terror and mystery—resides within.

Terrorism

Theirs and Ours

❀

EQBAL AHMAD

IN THE 1930S AND 1940S, the Jewish underground in Palestine was described as "terrorist." Then new things happened. By 1942, the Holocaust was occurring, and a certain liberal sympathy with the Jewish people had built up in the Western world. At that point, the terrorists of Palestine, who were Zionists, suddenly started to be described by 1944–1945 as "freedom fighters." At least two Israeli prime ministers, including Menachem Begin, have actually, you can find in the books, posters with their pictures, saying, "Terrorists, reward this much." The highest reward I have noted so far was 100,000 British pounds on the head of Menachem Begin the terrorist.

Then, from 1969 to 1990 the PLO, the Palestine Liberation Organization, occupied the center stage as the terrorist organization. Yasir Arafat has been described repeatedly by the great sage of American journalism, William Safire of the *New York Times*, as the "chief of terrorism." That's Yasir Arafat. Now, on September 29, 1998, I was rather amused to notice a picture of Yasir Arafat to the right of President Bill Clinton. To his left is Israeli Prime Minister Benjamin Netanyahu. Clinton is looking towards Arafat and Arafat is looking literally like a meek mouse. Just a few years earlier, he used to appear with this very menacing look around him, with a gun appearing menacing from his belt. You remember those pictures, and you remember the next one.

In 1985, President Ronald Reagan received a group of bearded men. I was writing about these bearded men in those days in *The New Yorker*. They were very ferocious-looking bearded men with turbans, looking like they came from another century. President Reagan received them in the White House. After receiving them, he spoke to the press. He pointed towards them, I'm sure some of you will recall that moment, and said, "These are the moral equivalent of America's founding fathers." These were the Afghan *mujahiddin*. They were at the time, guns in hand, battling the Evil Empire. They were the moral equivalent of our founding fathers.

In August 1998, another American president ordered missile strikes from the American navy, based in the Indian Ocean, to kill Osama bin Laden and his men in the camps in Afghanistan. I do not wish to embarrass you with the reminder that Mr. bin Laden, whom fifteen American missiles were fired to hit in Afghanistan, was only a few years ago the moral equivalent of George Washington and Thomas Jefferson. He got angry over the fact that he has been demoted from moral equivalent of your founding fathers, so he is taking out his anger in different ways. I'll come back to that subject more seriously in a moment.

You see why I have recalled all these stories is to point out to you that the matter of terrorism is rather complicated. Terrorists change. The terrorist of yesterday is the hero of today, and the hero of yesterday becomes the terrorist of today. This is a serious matter of constantly changing world of images in which we have to keep our heads straight to know what is terrorism and what is not. But more importantly, to know what causes it and how to stop it.

The next point about our terrorism is that posture of inconsistency necessarily evades definition. If you are not going to be consistent, you're not going to define.

I have examined at least twenty official documents on terrorism. Not one defines the word. All of them explain it, express it emotively, polemically, to arouse our emotions, rather than exercise our intelligence. I give you only one example, which is representative. October 25, 1984. George Shultz, then secretary of state of the U.S., is speaking at the New York Park Avenue Synagogue. It's a long speech on terrorism. In the State Department Bulletin of seven, single-spaced pages, there is not a single definition of terrorism. What we get is the following: "Terrorism is a modern barbarism that we call terrorism." Definition number one. Definition number two is even more brilliant: "Terrorism is a form of political violence." Aren't you surprised? It is a form of political violence, says George Shultz, secretary of state of the U.S. Number three: "Terrorism is a threat to Western civilization." Number four: "Terrorism is a menace to Western moral values." Did you notice, does it tell you anything other than arouse your emotions? This is typical.

They don't define terrorism because definitions involve a commitment to analysis, comprehension, and adherence to some norms of consistency. That's the second characteristic of the official literature on terrorism. The third characteristic is that the absence of definition does not prevent officials from being globalistic. We may not define terrorism, but it is a menace to the moral values of Western civilization. It is a menace also to mankind. It's a menace to good order. Therefore, you must stamp it out worldwide. Our reach has to be global. You need a global reach to kill it. Antiterrorist policies, therefore, have to be global. Same speech of George Shultz: "There is no question about our ability to use force where and when it is needed to counter terrorism." There is no geographical limit. On a single day, the missiles hit Afghanistan and Sudan. Those two countries are 2,300 miles apart, and they were hit by missiles belonging to a country roughly 8,000 miles away. Reach is global.

A fourth characteristic: Claims of power are not only globalist, they are also omniscient. We know where they are, therefore we know where to hit. We have the means to know. We have the instruments of knowledge. We are omniscient. Shultz: "We know the difference between terrorists and freedom fighters, and as we look around, we have no trouble telling one from the other." Only Osama bin Laden doesn't know that he was an ally one day and an enemy another. That's very confusing for Osama bin Laden. I'll come back to his story towards the end. It's a real story.

Five. The official approach eschews causation. You don't look at causes of anybody becoming terrorist. Cause? What cause? They ask us to be looking, to be sympathetic to these people. Another example. The *New York Times*, December 18, 1985, reported that the foreign minister of Yugoslavia, you remember the days when there was a Yugoslavia, requested the secretary of state of the U.S. to consider the causes of Palestinian terrorism. The secretary of state, George Shultz, and I'm quoting from the *New York Times*, "went a bit red in the face. He pounded the table and told the visiting foreign minister, 'There is no connection with any cause. Period.'" Why look for causes?

Number six. The moral revulsion that we must feel against terrorism is selective. We are to feel the terror of those groups that are officially disapproved. We are to applaud the terror of those groups of whom officials do approve. Hence, President Reagan, I am a *contra*. He actually said that. We know the *contras* of Nicaragua were anything by any definition but terrorists. The media, to move away from the officials, heed the dominant view of terrorism.

The dominant approach also excludes from consideration, more importantly to me, the terror of friendly governments. To that question I will return, because it excused among others the terror of Pinochet, who killed one of my closest friends, Orlando Letelier, and it excused the terror of Zia ul-Haq, who killed many of my friends in Pakistan. All I want to tell you is that, according to my ignorant calculations, the ratio of people killed by the state terror of Zia ul-Haq, Pinochet, Argentinian, Brazilian, Indonesian type, versus the killing of the PLO and other terrorist types is literally, conservatively, one to one hundred thousand. That's the ratio.

History unfortunately recognizes and accords visibility to power and not to weakness. Therefore, visibility has been accorded historically to dominant groups. In our time, the time that began with *this* day, Columbus Day, the time that begins with Columbus Day is a time of extraordinary unrecorded holocausts. Great civilizations have been wiped out. The Mayas, the Incas, the Aztecs, the American Indians, the Canadian Indians were all wiped out. Their voices have not been heard, even to this day fully. Now they are beginning to be heard, but not fully. They are heard, yes, but only when the dominant power suffers, only when resistance has a semblance of costing, of exacting a price, when a Custer is killed or when a Gordon is besieged. That's when you know that they were Indians fighting, Arabs fighting and dying.

My last point of this section. U.S. policy in the Cold War period has sponsored terrorist regimes one after another. Somoza, Batista, all kinds of tyrants have been America's friends. You know that. There was a reason for that. I or you are not guilty. Nicaragua, *contra*. Afghanistan, *mujahiddin*. El Salvador, and so on.

Now the second side. You've suffered enough. So suffer more.

There ain't much good on the other side either. You shouldn't imagine that I have come to praise the other side. But keep the balance in mind. Keep the imbalance in mind and first ask ourselves, What is terrorism? Our first job should be to define the damn thing, name it, give it a description of some kind, other than "moral equivalent of founding fathers" or "a moral outrage to Western civilization." I will stay with you with Webster's Collegiate Dictionary: "Terror is an intense, overpowering fear." He uses terrorizing, terrorism, "the use of terrorizing methods of governing or resisting a government." This simple definition has one great virtue, that of fairness. It's fair. It focuses on the use of coerce violence, violence that is used illegally, extraconstitutionally, to coerce. And this definition is correct because it treats terror for what it is, whether the government or private people commit it.

Have you noticed something? Motivation is left out of it. We're not talking about whether the cause is just or unjust. We're talking about consensus, consent, absence of consent, legality, absence of legality, constitutionality, absence of constitutionality. Why do we keep motives out? Because motives differ. Motives differ and make no difference. I have identified in my work five types of terrorism. First, state terrorism, second, religious terrorism, terrorism inspired by religion, Catholics killing Protestants, Sunnis killing Shiites, Shiites killing Sunnis, God, religion, sacred terror, you can call it if you wish. State, church, crime. Mafia. All kinds of crime commit terror. There is pathology. You're pathological. You're sick. You want the attention of the whole world. You've got to kill a president. You will. You terrorize. You hold up a bus. Fifth, there is political terror of the private group, be they Indian, Vietnamese, Algerian, Palestinian, Baader-Meinhof, the Red Brigade. Political terror of the private group. Oppositional terror. Keep these five in mind. Keep in mind one more thing. Sometimes these five can converge on each other. You start with protest terror. You go crazy. You become pathological. You continue.

They converge. State terror can take the form of private terror. For example, we're all familiar with the death squads in Latin America or in Pakistan. Government has employed private people to kill its opponents. It's not quite official. It's privatized. Convergence. Or the political terrorist who goes crazy and becomes pathological. Or the criminal who joins politics. In Afghanistan, in Central America, the CIA employed in its covert operations drug pushers. Drugs and guns often go together. Smuggling of all things often go together.

Of the five types of terror, the focus is on only one, the least important in terms of cost to human lives and human property. The highest cost is state terror. The second highest cost is religious terror, although in the twentieth century religious terror has, relatively speaking, declined. If you are looking historically, massive costs. The next highest cost is crime. Next highest, pathology. A Rand Corporation study by Brian Jenkins, for a ten-year period up to 1988, showed 50% of terror was committed without any political cause at all. No politics. Simply crime and pathology. So the focus is on only one, the political terrorist, the PLO, the bin Laden, whoever you want to take. Why do they do it? What makes the terrorist tick?

I would like to knock them out quickly to you. First, the need to be heard. Imagine, we are dealing with a minority group, the political, private terrorist. First, the need to be heard. Normally, and there are exceptions, there is an effort to be heard, to get your grievances heard by people. They're not hearing it. A minority acts. The majority applauds. The Palestinians, for example, the superterrorists of our time, were dispossessed in 1948. From 1948 to 1968 they went to every court in the world. They knocked at every door in the world. They were told that they became dispossessed because some radio told them to go away, an Arab radio, which was a lie. Nobody was listening to the truth. Finally, they invented a new form of terror, literally their invention: the airplane hijacking. Between 1968 and 1975 they pulled the world up by its ears. They dragged us out, said, Listen, listen. We listened. We still haven't done them justice, but at least we all know. Even the Israelis acknowledge. Remember Golda Meir, Prime Minister of Israel, saying in 1970, There are no Palestinians. They do not exist. They damn well exist now. We are cheating them at Oslo. At least there are some people to cheat now. We can't just push them out. The need to be heard is essential. One motivation there.

Mix of anger and helplessness produces an urge to strike out. You are angry. You are feeling helpless. You want retribution. You want to wreak retributive justice. The experience of violence by a stronger party has historically turned victims into terrorists. Battered children are known to become abusive parents and violent adults. You know that. That's what happens to peoples and nations. When they are battered, they hit back. State terror very often breeds collective terror. Do you recall the fact that the Jews were never terrorists? By and large Jews were not known to commit terror except during and after the Holocaust. Most studies show that the majority of members of the worst terrorist groups in Israel or in Palestine, the Stern and the Irgun gangs, were people who were immigrants from the most anti-Semitic countries of Eastern Europe and Germany. Similarly, the young Shiites of Lebanon or the Palestinians from the refugee camps are battered people. They become very violent. The ghettos are violent internally. They become violent externally when there is a clear, identifiable external target, an enemy where you can say, Yes, this one did it to me. Then they can strike back.

Example is a bad thing. Example spreads. There was a highly publicized Beirut hijacking of the TWA plane. After that hijacking, there were hijacking attempts at nine different American airports. Pathological groups or individuals modeling on the others. Even more serious are examples set by governments. When governments engage in terror, they set very large examples. When they engage in supporting terror, they engage in other sets of examples.

Absence of revolutionary ideology is central to victim terrorism. Revolutionaries do not commit unthinking terror. Those of you who are familiar with revolutionary theory know the debates, the disputes, the quarrels, the fights within revolutionary groups of Europe, the fight between anarchists and Marxists, for example. But the Marxists have always argued that revolutionary terror, if ever engaged in, must be sociologically and psychologically selective. Don't hijack a plane. Don't hold hostages. Don't kill children, for God's sake. Have you recalled also that the great revolutions, the Chinese, the Vietnamese, the Algerian, the Cuban, never engaged in hijacking type of terrorism? They did engage in terrorism, but it was highly selective, highly sociological, still deplorable, but there was an organized, highly limited, selective character to it. So absence of revolutionary ideology that begins more or less in the post-World War II period, has been central to this phenomenon.

My final question is, These conditions have existed for a long time. But why then this flurry of private political terrorism? Why now so much of it and so visible? The answer is modern technology. You have a cause. You can communicate it through radio and television. They will all come swarming if you have taken an aircraft and are holding 150 Americans hostage. They will all hear your cause. You have a modern weapon through which you can shoot a mile away. They can't reach you. And you have the modern means of communicating. When you put together the cause, the instrument of coercion and the instrument of communication, politics is made. A new kind of politics becomes possible.

To this challenge rulers from one country after another have been responding with traditional methods. The traditional method of shooting it out, whether it's missiles or some other means. The Israelis are very proud of it. The Americans are very proud of it. The French became very proud of it. Now the Pakistanis are very proud of it. The Pakistanis say, Our commandos are the best. Frankly, it won't work. A central problem of our time, political minds, rooted in the past, and modern times, producing new realities. Therefore in conclusion, what is my recommendation to America?

Quickly, what to do. First, avoid extremes of double standards. If you're going to practice double standards, you will be paid with double standards. Don't use it. Don't condone Israeli terror, Pakistani terror, Nicaraguan terror, El Salvadoran terror, on the one hand, and then complain about Afghan terror or Palestinian terror. It doesn't work. Try to be even-handed. A superpower cannot promote terror in one place and reasonably expect to discourage terrorism in another place. It won't work in this shrunken world.

Do not condone the terror of your allies. Condemn them. Fight them. Punish them. Please eschew, avoid covert operations and low-intensity warfare. These are breeding grounds of terror and drugs. Violence and drugs are bred there. The structure of covert operations, I've made a film about it that has been very popular in Europe, called *Dealing with the Demon*. I have shown that wherever covert operations have been, there has been the central drug problem. That has been also the center of the drug trade. Because the structure of covert operations, Afghanistan, Vietnam, Nicaragua, Central America, is very hospitable to drug trade. Avoid it. Give it up. It doesn't help.

Please focus on causes and help ameliorate causes. Try to look at causes and solve problems. Do not concentrate on military solutions. Do not seek military solutions. Terrorism is a political problem. Seek political solutions. Diplomacy works. Take the example of the last attack on bin Laden. You don't know what you're attacking. They say they know, but they don't know. They were trying to kill Qadaffi. They killed his four-year-old daughter. The poor baby hadn't done anything. Qadaffi is still alive. They tried to kill Saddam Hussein. They killed Laila bin Attar, a prominent artist, an innocent woman. They tried to kill bin Laden and his men. Not one but twenty-five other people died. They tried to destroy a chemical factory in Sudan. Now they are admitting that they destroyed an innocent factory, one-half of the production of medicine in Sudan has been destroyed, not a chemical factory. You don't know. You think you know.

Four of your missiles fell in Pakistan. One was slightly damaged. Two were totally damaged. One was totally intact. For ten years the American government has kept an embargo on Pakistan because Pakistan is trying, stupidly, to build nuclear weapons and missiles. So we have a technology embargo on my country. One of the missiles was intact. What do you think the Pakistani official told the *Washington Post*? He said it was a gift from Allah. [laughter] We wanted U.S. technology. Now we have got the technology, and our scientists are examining this missile very carefully. It fell into the wrong hands. So don't do that. Look for political solutions. Do not look for military solutions. They cause more problems than they solve.

Please help reinforce, strengthen the framework of international law. There was a criminal court in Rome. Why didn't they go to it first to get their warrant against bin Laden, if they have some evidence? Get a warrant, then go after him. Internationally. Enforce the U.N. Enforce the International Court of Justice, this unilateralism makes us look very stupid and them relatively smaller.

Q & A

The question here is that I mentioned that I would go somewhat into the story of bin Laden, the Saudi in Afghanistan and didn't do so, could I go into some detail? The point about bin Laden would be roughly the same as the point between Sheikh Abdul Rahman, who was accused and convicted of encouraging the blowing up of the World Trade Center in New York City. *The New Yorker* did a long story on him. It's the same as that of Aimal Kansi, the Pakistani Baluch who was also convicted of the murder of two CIA agents. Let me see if I can be very short on this. *Jihad*, which has been translated a thousand times as "holy war," is not quite just that. Jihad is an Arabic word that means "to struggle." It could be struggle by violence or struggle by nonviolent means. There are two forms, the small jihad and the big jihad. The small jihad involves violence. The big jihad involves the struggles with self. Those are the concepts. The reason I mention it is that in Islamic history, jihad as an international violent phenomenon had disappeared in the last four hundred years, for all practical purposes. It was revived suddenly with American help in the 1980s. When the Soviet Union intervened in Afghanistan, Zia ul-Haq, the military dictator of Pakistan, which borders on Afghanistan, saw an opportunity and launched a jihad there against godless communism. The U.S. saw a God-sent opportunity to mobilize one billion Muslims against what Reagan called the Evil Empire. Money started pouring in. CIA agents starting going all over the Muslim world recruiting people to fight in the great jihad. Bin Laden was one of the early prize recruits. He was not only an Arab. He was also a Saudi. He was not only a Saudi. He was also a multimillionaire, willing to put his own money into the matter. Bin Laden went around recruiting people for the jihad against communism.

I first met him in 1986. He was recommended to me by an American official of whom I do not know whether he was or was not an agent. I was talking to him and said, Who are the Arabs here who would be very interesting? By here I meant in Afghanistan and Pakistan. He said, You must meet Osama. I went to see Osama. There he was, rich, bringing in recruits from Algeria, from Sudan, from Egypt, just like Sheikh Abdul Rahman. This fellow was an ally. He remained an ally. He turns at a particular moment. In 1990 the U.S. goes into Saudi Arabia with forces. Saudi Arabia is the holy place of Muslims, Mecca and Medina. There had never been foreign troops there. In 1990, during the Gulf War, they went in in the name of helping Saudi Arabia defeat Saddam

Hussein. Osama bin Laden remained quiet. Saddam was defeated, but the American troops stayed on in the land of the *kaba* (the sacred site of Islam in Mecca), foreign troops. He wrote letter after letter saying, Why are you here? Get out! You came to help but you have stayed on. Finally he started a jihad against the other occupiers. His mission is to get American troops out of Saudi Arabia. His earlier mission was to get Russian troops out of Afghanistan. See what I was saying earlier about covert operations?

A second point to be made about him is these are tribal people, people who are really tribal. Being a millionaire doesn't matter. Their code of ethics is tribal. The tribal code of ethics consists of two words: loyalty and revenge. You are my friend. You keep your word. I am loyal to you. You break your word, I go on my path of revenge. For him, America has broken its word. The loyal friend has betrayed. The one to whom you swore blood loyalty has betrayed you. They're going to go for you. They're going to do a lot more. These are the chickens of the Afghanistan war coming home to roost. This is why I said to stop covert operations. There is a price attached to those that the American people cannot calculate and Kissinger type of people do not know, don't have the history to know. [applause]

This Alternative Radio interview of Eqbal Ahmad with David Barsamian was conducted when Ahmad was professor emeritus of International Relations and Middle Eastern Studies at Hampshire College in Amherst, Massachusetts. For many years, he was managing editor of the quarterly Race and Class. *His articles and essays appeared in* The Nation *and other journals throughout the world. Ahmad died in Islamabad, Pakistan, on May 11, 1999. His close friend, Edward Said, wrote, "He was perhaps the shrewdest and most original anti-imperialist analyst of the postwar world." Interview copyright © 1998 David Barsamian.*

As We Grieve . . . What Shall We Do?

❁

PETER SCHMIECHEN

IT IS NOW TWELVE DAYS since the day of terror in New York City, the Pentagon, and Somerset County. Things are moving so quickly that these words, written five days ago, may need revision by the time you read them. We have been overwhelmed by the magnitude of the human loss and destruction of property. The images of suffering and death, fear and grief, are in our heads and hearts. Many people in Lancaster have relatives and friends in the devastation or surrounding communities. We grasped for hope that it might not be so bad, only to find that it was. The full impact of it hit me when I asked if New York had adequate medical personnel to tend the wounded. The reply I got was that, after the initial wave of wounded, there are no more wounded.

So we now live in what the media are calling a post-September 11 world, where the reality of international violence and warfare has come to our nation and has shattered the lives of thousands. In such a world, we are confronted with issues that we either ignored or tucked away, only to discuss them in rather controlled settings: Is there any security from such terror? Whom can we trust? What is really important and worth defending? What do I do with my fear and sorrow? And, of course, what shall we do — individually and as a nation?

The media and the government are pressing for answers. But I must confess that I find myself, and so many people, in such a state of shock that we may need more time to deal with our initial reactions of grief and anger before we can reflect with genuine clarity. Knowing who actually did this would also help, as would a great deal more information about security systems and the kind of dangers already before us. Like you, I will be more than interested in jumping into the debates over the moral, social, and political aspects of this. But grieving and learning the truth might have to come first. What we don't need is careless blaming. The kinds of statements that came from Jerry Falwell and Pat Robertson are indeed reckless. To blame a terrorist-event on the people in the America they do not like is a hateful act. The Bible interprets catastrophes in a variety of ways, and one is, indeed, that they are a judgment from God. But it is not self-evident when this latter interpretation should be applied. To suggest this is an act of God makes God a terrorist. Obviously, the event has exposed our vulnerability, and it is easy to lament lax systems and complacency. Each day, the government announces changes in security systems and warns of new stringency. We have been reluctant to tighten controls. In a culture that cannot prevent children from killing one another in schools, it is difficult to stop suicide terrorists.

As we grieve and take care of victims and their families, what shall we do? Consider this: First, take time to consider what is really important. I am struck by the fact that in the last minute phone calls from people in the buildings and on planes, they called to say:

"I love you." Such testimonials reveal a final affirmation of what is important. Perhaps we might engage in a new discussion on what we take to be essential in our individual and national life. When we declare that now is the time to preserve our way of life, what specifically do we mean?

Second, let us show respect for our Anabaptist brothers and sisters who, I am sure, will quietly abstain from sanctioning military action. No matter how certain one is that military action is justified, remember that it is never applied in a perfect way. The means and passions of war are difficult to control. Luther said that "War is like fishing with a golden net: the potential loss is always greater than the gain." The witness from Anabaptists and others opposed to military action needs to be heard, which leads to the past point: No matter how righteous our cause and great our resolve, there are still limits to what we may do. Good intentions do not justify everything. We cannot forget the distinction between intentions and strategies. Americans are loyal, but not blind. We may agree that terrorism must be stopped, but we also need to evaluate how this is to be done. Every war in the last century was followed by vigorous debates over the effectiveness and morality of particular strategies. Even in war, we are accountable to one another and to God. We cannot act in a way wherein we become the very thing we oppose. The hate crimes against people from the Middle East and India are already an example of how moral outrage becomes immoral. Let us pray for our leaders and support them. Let us pray that they will choose wisely those strategies that will, in the long run, create justice and peace, here and throughout the world.

Peter Schmiechen has recently retired as president of Lancaster Theological Seminary.

Reprinted from *The Lancaster Sunday News*, September 2001. Used by permission.

A Time for Stories

※

TOM EHRICH

OUR TRAINING EVENT and lighthearted mood ended instantly when a trainee fielded a call from Pittsburgh and informed us, "Terrorists attacked the World Trade Center!"

A trainee from Manhattan ran to a pay phone at our hotel near Washington, D.C. I joined dozens watching CNN's remarkable video of 110-story towers burning and crumbling.

We watched flames engulf the Pentagon—just down the road, grim and sobering.

Time to go home. Time to stand with our families. We packed up our computers, marveled at how peaceful suburban Maryland looked, and charted a city-avoiding route home.

The Shenandoah Valley of Virginia looked lovely and unchanged. In a Burger King, patrons watched CNN and exchanged muted assurances over Whoppers.

For eight hours, we listened to National Public Radio. We needed to know whether our government was still functioning. We needed to know if a next wave of attacks had begun.

Rumors came and went. Remaining and deepening, however, was the horror. Firemen and policemen died as they raced into danger. Hospital triage centers set up in the hope that there would be living people to triage, not just bodies to tag. People choosing to jump ninety stories rather than burn. The Pentagon torn open. A fourth crash near Pittsburgh. Some politicians sounding small and unreliable.

I found my family at soccer practice. My little boy was racing to defend his goal from an attacker dribbling a ball. My wife and I exchanged a hug deeper than the usual welcome-home embrace. Our older sons—draft age—checked in. I called my parents.

At home, my son did his homework, preparing for a future that now looks different. I remembered teaching his class last Friday how America could build its cities in the open, because we have lived at peace with our neighbors and not had to deal with foreign attacks. Today, aircraft carriers are stationed offshore.

Too many questions: Are we at war? Who is our enemy? Will our leaders know how to respond? Will the economy nosedive? Will a populace unaccustomed to sacrifice turn bitter, hostile to immigrants, and vengeful? Will we find those bedrock values and freedoms cited in the day's hastily crafted speeches?

It is, I believe, a time for stories—to recount where we were when we heard, to know our feelings, to listen to each other, and to wonder aloud. It is a time to remain in the open, not to hide.

It will be a time for conflict. Missiles will fly, troops will move, more will die. Some warfare will happen far from home, with a few brave men and women on site and most of us watching CNN. But now a line has been crossed—a line we had not known was so easily crossed—and our own soil faces danger.

I doubt that it is a time for large and important words. We need facts, not profundity. We need measured and wise action, not rage and a rush to retaliate. We need to separate what we know from what we fear. We need to give blood, shelter strangers, save the wounded, honor the dead, and protect the Islamic in our midst from becoming scapegoats.

We need to honor our soldiers and sailors, whose underpaid lives will be laid on the line.

Politicians will turn to blaming. It seems all they know how to do. Headline-seekers will leak information; those with a taste for demagoguery will point accusing fingers. Some will pick up the president's language of good vs. evil. Rhetoric will escalate.

Christians will speak with many voices, some frighteningly certain. We are masters at blaming. We know the good-vs.-evil gambit. We know the conviction that motivates the Osama bin Ladens of this world. We, too, have killed in the name of God. We have destroyed lives in pursuit of right opinion. We have enshrined hatred. We have ignored how Jesus welcomed sinners and ate with his enemies.

We, of all people, should be reciting psalms and telling stories, not mounting our pulpits. We know too well the horror that can come from righteous wrath.

Tom Ehrich is a writer and computer consultant, managing large-scale database implementations. An Episcopal priest, he lives in Durham, North Carolina.

Response to the Events of September 11

❀

MARK J. STEWART

WHEN THE TRAGIC EVENTS of September 11 unfolded, I knew that I would be called to active duty. I am a chaplain assigned to Dover Air Force Base, Delaware, where the only military-port mortuary for the nation is located. It was here that all of the victims of the Pentagon crash were taken for identification purposes. In all my years of training, nothing prepared me for what I experienced firsthand during this mass casualty. In many ways, it didn't seem real, but sights and smells told me otherwise. I will say that no one who participates in such an event walks away unchanged. I am not the same person I was before September 11. I will not put a value on this change — it just is. Shattered lives and charred remains have a way of doing this to you.

While I was at Dover, I was a part of three separate teams designed to provide services to those persons immediately handling the remains. At times, I met the delivery flights coming into the base. Each reception of remains was given the utmost respect and dignity. This is important to remember because the remains of innocent victims and terrorists were indistinguishable. While on the flight line, I offered a prayer over the remains and provided counsel to other team members. I was also on the Critical Incident Stress Management and mortuary teams. These responsibilities included providing pastoral support and counsel to the 250 men and women working at the mortuary. These included military members, National Safety Transportation Board representatives, and FBI agents. Some of them had never performed this duty before. I hold a deeper appreciation for not only all of them but for the many emergency workers who face problems great and small on a daily basis.

While the work went smoothly, it was not without incident. Overall, though, there was a resiliency in the American spirit to see this tragic moment through. It was a time for all of us to remember the fragility of life, to touch base with our own faith, and to step boldly into an uncertain new life. I was fortunate to work with a dedicated and supportive leadership. Twenty-seven chaplain assistants and chaplains quickly melded into a team. This, in spite of the fact that we came from bases around the United States and that one chaplain had lost at least twenty-seven members of his congregation in the World Trade Center crashes. The support we gave to others was the same support we gave to one another out of our various traditions.

On a more personal note, I have faced M60 automatics and have undergone body and vehicle checks before, but having an M60 pointed at me on United States soil was disconcerting. Furthermore, entrance barriers required me to navigate around them to get where I needed to go. Parking areas on the base were restricted and removed from immediate buildings that were blacked out and locked. Signs everywhere were covered, and identification was required before being permitted into any building. It is only by the grace of God that we move and have our being. It is with hope that we step boldly in the future. A new spiritual awakening, sense of being and purpose, and dedication to principles of freedom and life has emerged from the carnage. Out of the shadow of death, there is a new morn. The United States is at war now, and I am on call for additional duty, if needed.

Mark J. Stewart is a chaplain and a major for the USAFR, Dover AFB, Delaware.

From *United Church News* (October 2001). Reprinted by permission.

Where Was the Church on September 11, 2001?

And What Are We Doing Now?

❀

STEPHANIE SPENCER

IN AFGHANISTAN, we had already been helping people affected by twenty-three years of war with emergency support to refugees and with health care and vocational training.

At Ground Zero, at the Pentagon, and in Pennsylvania, within hours, ministers trained in crisis counseling and church members trained in disaster response were offering support to rescue personnel who were working around the clock.

Around the U.S., as people saw the tragedies unfolding and wanted to help, they contributed to a special fund for people affected by the attacks.

Around the world, from the first few minutes after the towers collapsed, while the whole world watched on TV, emails and phone calls came from our Christian and Muslim sisters and brothers around the world, offering their shock and condolences.

WHAT WERE WE DOING?

Writing resources for reflection on 9-11 events and posting on the Web site and publishing them in the *UCNews*.

Writing reflections on the situation in Afghanistan, which was posted on the Web site and published in *UCNews* and *Common Lot*, the United Church of Christ's women's newsletter.

National staff were interviewed several times on local television to provide background on Afghanistan and the Middle East.

Writing a background article, "What Is Islam," for congregations that wanted to know more about this religion, which was posted on the Web site.

Organizing a workshop series for staff and community members introducing Islam, local Muslim leaders, and Christians with experience in interfaith work.

Producing a bulletin insert with 9-11 response resources, an Afghanistan information packet, and resources for worship, study, and reflection.

WHAT ARE WE DOING NOW?

Working on a study resource, "What is Terrorism," with ecumenical colleagues.

Providing workshops for church leaders in New York, New Jersey, Pennsylvania, Maryland, D.C., and Virginia to support them in their pastoral roles with congregations and families affected in the 9-11 attacks.

Working with other organizations to monitor the air quality at Ground Zero and to advocate for action by New York City and the EPA to clean up all the chemical pollutants there.

Assisting the surviving partners of lesbian and gay people to receive the financial support and other services available for family members affected by 9-11.

Working ecumenically for recovery and rebuilding in Afghanistan, providing tents, blankets, food, and supplies to rebuild houses destroyed by war; school supplies to children returning to school; and jobs for widows.

Finding churches that will help Afghan refugee families settle in the U.S. Most of these families have lived in refugee camps for ten to twenty years and can't go back to Afghanistan because their villages have been destroyed.

Learning skills for working with people in crisis through an internship in a UCC-related social service organization.

Learning about life in other parts of the world through a mission exposure trip or as a mission volunteer or intern.

Expressing opinions about the "war on terrorism" and about U.S. foreign policy to elected officials.

Learning more about the gifts that lesbian, gay, bisexual, and transgender Christians bring to the church.

Acting Globally and Locally

Twenty Things that Were Done and Can be Done to Make a Difference

❀

JUSTICE AND WITNESS MINISTRIES

Part of faithful response to tragedy is action. These are the kinds of things that can be and were done in the aftermath of September 11.

1. DECLARE YOUR HOME, office, church, store, and so on, an "Intolerance-Free Zone" by posting this message in your windows, which can be downloaded and reproduced on bright colored paper. A camera-ready copy of this sign has been included in the all-church mailing that will be mailed to your congregation on September 24. Share this sign with others in your neighborhood and community! Contact Justice and Witness Ministries if you want to receive this sign by mail.

2. Support immediate disaster relief through the United Church of Christ's "Hope from the Rubble" special appeal.

3. In order to alleviate suffering, confront evil, and promote peace throughout the next year, support the Neighbors in Need all-church offering scheduled for many congregations on World Communion Sunday, October 7, 2001, or whenever your congregation chooses to collect for Neighbors in Need.

4. Inform your congregation about the resources available for them on the United Church of Christ Web site. Some may not be aware of the information available at <www.ucc.org>.

5. Contact representatives of local Islamic centers to offer friendship and solidarity. Ask how you might partner with them to offer expressions of unity in your community. Participate in interfaith services.

6. If a mosque, synagogue, church, or community center is damaged or threatened in your area, take immediate steps to offer solidarity and support, as appropriate.

7. Remember that many smaller communities—even those without an organized Islamic presence—will likely have Arab-American residents. By speaking publicly and forcefully in your communities, you can forge new alliances and friendships for the sake of peace and justice.

8. Educate yourself and your congregation about Islam, Judaism, and Christianity. Ignorance only leads to false and misleading assumptions about the tenets of these major faiths. Learn more about these religions' teachings on peace and nonviolence.

9. Use symbolic gestures to not only express solidarity with fellow Americans but also to remember that this tragedy is global. Citizens of sixty-two nations were killed during the September 11 attack. The entire world is affected, so express concern for all God's children. Build unity for the sake of peace in your neighborhoods, communities, and cities.

10. Publicly decry any attempt to blame or scapegoat any single group or class of people for the tragedies of September 11.
11. Resist any call for revenge, retaliation, and further violence against groups of innocent people because of race, religion, or national ethnicity.
12. Raise the issue of Anti-Arab hate crimes publicly during your congregation's occasions of prayer and worship and during community-wide prayer services.
13. "Local Law Enforcement Enhancement Act" (S. 625 / H.R. 1343) known last year as the Hate Crimes Prevention Act, which has been introduced to the 107th Congress.
14. Find out about hate crimes and community responses in your area by logging on to <www.unitedagainsthate.org>.
15. Stop harassment of those who are or are perceived to be from the Middle East or are Muslim, if you witness it. If you are with others, you can surround that person with your bodies to keep the intimidators away.
16. If you are an Open and Affirming Church and have received threats, let your Conference Office know. If you are close to an Open and Affirming Church, or a Metropolitan Community Church, or other community of faith that welcomes gay, lesbian, bisexual, and transgendered people, check in with them to see if they are okay.
17. Be good to yourself. Take a break from the intensity of the news. Go to a movie. Take a walk in the park. Play with your kids. Sing. Maintain balance in this time of uncertainty and stress. For more suggestions, visit the *YES! Magazine* Web site: <www.yesmagazine.org>.
18. Go to church. Pray. Read scripture and search your heart and soul for understanding and solace. Understand your own anger and redirect it towards constructive activities. Talk with others and help each other express feelings and find ways to connect with positive action.
19. Reflect about the church's unique role in response to difficult issues like terrorism, violence, hate crimes, and war. What does it mean for the United Church of Christ to call itself a Just-Peace Church in times like these? Justice and Witness Ministries would love to hear your thoughts and perhaps share them with others. Send your written comments to <guessb@ucc.org>.
20. Remember your pressing urge to do something and channel your energy into promoting peace and unity in your own neighborhood and city. Do something now that will prevent acts of hatred in the future, even if you will never fully know the impact of your work. Your concrete actions for peace will change the world.

Rev. J. Bennett Guess is minister for communication and mission education for Justice and Witness Ministries, United Church of Christ.

Churches Open Doors for Prayers, Shelter

❀

KEVIN ECKSTROM

WASHINGTON—After reeling in despair from the terrorist bombings that killed thousands in New York and Washington, churches and houses of worship across the country opened their doors for prayer, an unprecedented public expression of collective grief and spiritual sensitivity.

As city streets emptied, church, synagogue, and mosque doors were swung open, with hastily made signs inviting people inside. At the National Shrine of the Immaculate Conception here, more than three thousand gathered Tuesday (September 11), with little notice, for Mass celebrated by Cardinal Theodore McCarrick.

In pews and silent chapels, parishioners shed tears of anguish and prayed for peace, evidence that the nation's emotional and spiritual scars may be deeper than her physical ones.

"Let us pray that this nightmare will soon be over," McCarrick said Wednesday during a packed Mass at St. Matthew's Cathedral downtown.

McCarrick ordered all parishes in the archdiocese of Washington to remain open for prayer and instructed priests to display the elements of the Eucharist for devotion. A similar appeal to open churches was issued by the bishops of the United Methodist Church and the archbishop of the Greek Orthodox Church.

In New York, Rev. Walter Tennyson of Broadway Presbyterian Church composed a special liturgy of prayer for a 1 P.M. service for passers-by, also opening the church as an overnight shelter.

Near disaster sites, churches opened their doors to the injured and the stranded. At Calvary United Methodist Church near the Pentagon, Pastor Steve Hassmer made the church available for stranded passengers at Washington's Reagan National Airport, offering phones to call home as well as prayer and counsel.

"We've been praying with people and giving them a chance to collect their thoughts as needed," Hassmer told United Methodist News Service, who added that most people were stranded subway passengers.

And just two blocks from the State Department, Western Presbyterian Church was transformed into an emergency day-care shelter for children of State Department employees. The church's pastor, Rev. John Wimberly, said the real challenge for Washington churches is yet to come.

"So many that go to our churches work for the federal government," he told Presbyterian News Service. "And suddenly, their workplace is a target. What's the psychological impact of that?"

As the dust settled and the reality of the trauma set in, religious leaders set about planning local prayer services, with several interfaith programs planned for major cities.

The Washington National Cathedral expects a citywide service within a week, and Georgetown University will host a special interfaith service with McCarrick on Thursday (September 13).

In Orange County, California, one of the nation's largest megachurches, Saddleback Church, opened its doors Tuesday to pray for "the Pearl Harbor of our generation."

The Union of American Hebrew Congregations, representing more than nine hundred Reform synagogues, issued suggested prayers and songs for interfaith services to be held in the coming weeks.

Church leaders also asked their congregants to help in practical terms, specifically pleading for monetary donations and blood. In Los Angeles, Catholic leaders set up a special disaster relief fund that will be sent directly to bishops in New York and Washington.

In New York, United Jewish Communities—the nation's umbrella organization for local Jewish federations—set up an emergency relief fund to aid families, communities, and relief agencies working in the aftermath.

I Now Wear My *Hijab* to Make My Personal Witness

❊

GABRIELLE CHAVEZ

RIGHT AFTER SEPTEMBER 11, I noticed how quickly the sight of women wearing Islamic dress, including the *hijab*, or headscarf, disappeared from our neighborhoods.

The last one I saw was on a woman attending an interfaith prayer service at Portland (Ore.) State University a week after the bombing.

Her name is Farsana, and she is from Bangladesh. I talked with her afterwards and asked her how to tie it. Because, by then, I had decided to begin wearing one myself.

Just to illustrate the vast difference in culture and religion this represents, the men in my life were not enthusiastic about my decision.

Thomas, my husband, said tactfully, "It doesn't flatter you." He also worried about me becoming a target of bigotry because, with Syrian ancestry, I could easily pass as an Arab woman.

My son, less tactful, asks me regularly when I am going to take it off again.

I don't know yet. I had to overcome a lot to put it on in the first place.

I confess it has always annoyed me to see Islamic women covering themselves up in our free country.

On top of that, I don't like scarves. They feel confining. They make me feel like my mother, who used to wear them when I was a child.

And they sure aren't flattering on me, that's true.

But Farsana almost cried with gratitude when I told her I was going to do it. That means a lot.

I wanted to take some action in response to the bombings, to make some personal witness to my faith in Christ's prayer, "that they all may be one."

And, I am not alone. Besides all who have been praying so faithfully, six of us (so far) from Christ the Healer UCC have volunteered to be available as escorts to women of the local Bilal mosque who now are afraid to go out shopping.

I find I can wear my *hijab* whenever I go out—fearlessly, if a bit self-consciously.

On a hospital visit, I think people just figured that I'm a cancer patient. At Costco, at the grocery store, or at the gas station, I get lots of looks and double takes, but so far, no unkindness.

The only place I didn't wear my *hijab*, ironically out of the same sensitivity that caused me to put one on in the first place, was to a Yom Kippur service.

At church, of course, I can count on people responding to me, not my scarf. Isn't that what the body of Christ is all about?

Gabrielle Chavez is co-convener with her husband, Thomas, of Christ the Healer UCC in Portland, Ore.

From *United Church News* on-line ed. <www.ucnews/dec01/inmy.htm>, December 2001. Reprinted by permission of Gabrielle Chavez.

TO LIVE PEACEABLY WITH ALL

Reflections on War and Peace

~

If it is possible,
so far as it depends on you,
live peaceably with all.

—Romans 12:18

~

IN THE UNITED CHURCH OF CHRIST, AS IN MOST AMERICAN CHURCHES, responses to the attacks on the Pentagon and the World Trade Center varied widely, even in the days immediately following the event. Some called for direct retaliatory action: "Bomb Afghanistan back into the Stone Age!" Others who had marched and protested against the "government's war" during the Vietnam era of the 1960s discovered the shallowness of their own pacifism: This was different. This required different strategies—if not full-scale war, then at least limited military action to bring the alleged perpetrators to justice. A few steadfastly maintained that violence always begets more violence and called for America's leaders to avoid the use of weapons of destruction altogether.

In 1985, the Fifteenth General Synod affirmed the United Church of Christ as a "Just Peace Church," a designation that encourages the active promotion of peace and justice within the constraints of reasonable self-defense. We are a denomination, the four Covenanted Ministry Boards of the denomination stated in a joint pastoral letter six months after the terrorists' attacks, that has a history of critiquing the "conventional wisdom" of the day. Not surprisingly, therefore, even in the first days of shock and mourning and anger, many comments and responses posted on the United Church of Christ Web site called not for vengeance and retribution but for justice with mercy. America's naïve serenity, its illusions of security and inviolability were shattered, perhaps permanently, by the events of September 11, 2001. Nevertheless, the faculty of one United Church of Christ seminary wrote in an open letter only ten days later, "Now is the time for Christians in particular to draw upon the deepest wellsprings of our religious heritage, remembering Jesus' words that 'whatsoever you do to the least of these my brothers and sisters, you do unto me.'"

Despite ongoing disagreements about the right means to combat global terrorism, church members continue to pray, to work diligently for peace, and to safeguard justice, even as they seek to understand the root causes of unrest and violence.

Jesus Said: "Blessed Are the Merciful"

❀

THE FACULTY OF ANDOVER NEWTON THEOLOGICAL SCHOOL

FACULTY AT THE UCC-RELATED ANDOVER NEWTON THEOLOGICAL SCHOOL near Boston have felt the same anguish and helplessness all of us have experienced in the past week. The two jets that smashed into the World Trade Center and the plane that crashed in Pennsylvania were hijacked after taking off from Boston Logan Airport, and many from the Boston area were aboard. This is a statement the faculty wanted to share with you:

In the shadows of war during the last century, theologian Reinhold Niebuhr wrote a prayer familiar to many: "God grant us the serenity to accept the things we cannot change, the courage to change the things we can, and the wisdom to know the difference." Such a prayer still speaks to us today amid the tragedies of recent days and public calls for retaliation. The shocking events of Tuesday's brutal attacks have forced on our nation a new awareness of our vulnerability to the violence of terrorism. The terrible images of destruction, now vividly etched in our minds, are ones that we would all like to change but cannot. They have become part of our national consciousness, immersing us with the world in sorrow, confusion, and anger. We join with all of those who are mourning the loss of innocent loved ones, colleagues, and friends in the atrocities directed against our nation: those who died in the planes and the dead and wounded of New York City and the Pentagon.

The courageous work of so many people, trained professionals and volunteers, who have offered help in past days testifies to the deepest strengths of our national character. Such acts and not threats of vengeance remain the most eloquent and effective witness we can make as Americans to the values and responsibilities of what it means to live as a free and democratic society.

Amid the escalating language voicing threats of war that have been expressed throughout our nation, we join those calling for restraint and proper reflection in these difficult times. We know that the witness of a just peace is stronger, in the long run, than the instruments of revenge. We know that the work of restoring our common life as a nation and within our communities demands more of us than the immediate satisfaction offered by retaliation, just as this finally requires more than the reconstruction of bricks and mortar alone. This work will call on us to build trust across the distances separating us by race and ethnic identity, religious and political difference, not only on the international scene but in the neighborhoods of our cities and towns, in the public square, and in communities of faith.

Now is the time for mourning and the immediate work of restoring order. Justice must have its day, but vengeance and violent retribution are not the means of attaining it. Now is the time to stand in solidarity with all our neighbors and demonstrate to the world that such trust is the very foundation on which a free democracy stands. Only such trust alone is finally unassailable by acts of terrorist aggression.

Serenity in these days will seem unattainable for many of us. But the wisdom of restraint is within our reach. This is not the time for cursory pronouncements of vengeance and hasty promises of retribution. This is the time for generosity toward the most vulnerable: the families and survivors of the victims of these atrocities and those displaced from their homes in the wake of these acts, of course. But also those innocent citizens and guests among us, particularly those of Arab descent, whose well-being and safety are threatened by angry prejudice and the escalating rhetoric of retaliation, both on the national and local scene.

Now is the time for Christians, in particular, to draw upon the deepest wellsprings of our religious heritage, remembering Jesus' words that "whatsoever you do to the least of these my brothers and sisters, you do unto me." Now is the time for all of us, regardless of religious affiliation, to heed the hard but healing words of Jesus' promise when he said, "Blessed are the merciful, for they shall obtain mercy."

The Faculty of Andover Newton Theological School
Newton Centre, Massachusetts 02459

Written and delivered at a campus prayer vigil, Andover Newton Theological School, September 14, 2001. Reprinted by permission of Elizabeth Nordbeck.

A Statement by the Collegium of Officers
of the United Church of Christ

❀

DALE BISHOP, EDITH A. GUFFEY,
BERNICE POWELL JACKSON, JOSÉ A. MALAYANG,
AND JOHN H. THOMAS

THE INITIATION OF MILITARY ACTION by the United States of America against Afghanistan opens a painful and dangerous new chapter in the tragic story that began a month ago in New York, Washington, and Pennsylvania. As we wept over the images of fallen towers in nearby New York, we now weep over scenes of death and destruction in distant Kabul. As we held our own children close during the frightening hours of terrorist attack, we now tremble for vulnerable children and innocent refugees who are in danger of bombs and starvation. As Christians, we confess that violence has been met by further violence, that we have turned from the way of the Cross to the way of the sword, that God's intentions are once again denied, that the vision of just peace remains elusive in a world fascinated by military might. There can be no joy for us this week, only lament. **Lord, have mercy.**

Every human being has a right to be free from the threat of terror. The fear we experience is very real, yet as Christians we also know it must not control us. Faithful people will not all agree on how best to provide that security in the midst of a dangerous world. Many members of the United Church of Christ support military action, believing it is the only way to achieve security for ourselves and for others. While we recognize that the rule of law must be enforced, we have grave reservations about a large-scale military response to terrorism by our government and its allies. In recent years, military campaigns in countless places have destroyed lives and threatened a whole generation of children while leaving in place oppressive regimes. Short-term solutions have sown the seeds of future catastrophe as we ally ourselves with the enemies of our enemy, only to discover that we have fed and armed those who would terrorize the innocent. Meanwhile, we have distanced ourselves from the Palestinian-Israeli conflict, have ignored civil wars in Africa, have done little to address the poverty and hunger that is the primary terror for most in the world, and have supplied countless regimes with abundant weaponry. Nothing justifies terrorist violence. The brutal attacks of September 11 cannot be blamed on God or on the failures of our own nation's policies. The attacks remain the responsibility of those who planned them and carried them out, and they must be brought to justice. Yet, we must confess that we have contributed to the poverty, the militarism, and the regional instability that have provided hospitable environments and comfortable havens for those who resort to violence. **Christ, have mercy.**

Our nation's leaders have set a course that meets violence with violence. Our lament over this decision does not deny our grief for those who have died, our love for this land, or the earnestness of our prayer, "God bless America." But our prayers also join this prayer for all who are put at risk by this course, both those who will be killed in these attacks and those who carry them out. May our nation's decision to go to war be matched now by a desire to use the even more massive nonviolent power available to us to address those chronic conflicts that destabilize the world; to fight the hunger and poverty that kill thousands every day; to find homes for the refugees on every continent; to defend the human rights of all who are oppressed because of their race, their political convictions, their gender, or their religion; and to create hope for families just as precious in God's sight as our own. May those of us whose baptism marks us with the sign of the Cross bear witness to the way of forgiveness, that we might become signs and instruments of God's design. May we learn again that true security is a gift we receive, a comfort we know in belonging to Christ. And may these tragic days move us to an ever more profound experience of the ancient plea, **"Lord, have mercy."**

Deny Them Their Victory

A Religious Response to Terrorism

❀

ENDORSED BY MORE THAN 3800 CHRISTIAN,
MUSLIM, AND JEWISH LEADERS DURING THE DAYS
FOLLOWING THE EVENTS OF SEPTEMBER 11

WE, AMERICAN RELIGIOUS LEADERS, share the broken hearts of our fellow citizens. The worst terrorist attack in history that assaulted New York City, Washington, D.C., and Pennsylvania, has been felt in every American community. Each life lost was of unique and sacred value in the eyes of God, and the connections Americans feel to those lives run very deep.

In the face of such a cruel catastrophe, it is a time to look to God and to each other for the strength we need and the response we will make. We must dig deep to the roots of our faith for sustenance, solace, and wisdom.

First, we must find a word of consolation for the untold pain and suffering of our people. Our congregations will offer their practical and pastoral resources to bind up the wounds of the nation. We can become safe places to weep and secure places to begin rebuilding our shattered lives and communities. Our houses of worship should become public arenas for common prayer, community discussion, eventual healing, and forgiveness.

Second, we offer a word of sober restraint as our nation discerns what its response will be. We share the deep anger toward those who so callously and massively destroy innocent lives, no matter what the grievances or injustices invoked.

In the name of God, we, too, demand that those responsible for these utterly evil acts be found and brought to justice. Those culpable must not escape accountability. But we must not, out of anger and vengeance, indiscriminately retaliate in ways that bring on even more loss of innocent life. We pray that President Bush and members of Congress will seek the wisdom of God as they decide upon the appropriate response.

Third, we face deep and profound questions of what this attack on America will do to us as a nation. The terrorists have offered us a stark view of the world they would create, where the remedy to every human grievance and injustice is a resort to the random and cowardly violence of revenge—even against the most innocent. Having taken thousands of our lives, attacked our national symbols, forced our political leaders to flee their chambers of governance, disrupted our work and families, and struck fear into the hearts of our children, the terrorists must feel victorious.

But we can deny them their victory by refusing to submit to a world created in their image. Terrorism inflicts not only death and destruction but also emotional oppression to further its aims. We must not allow this terror to drive us away from being the people

God has called us to be. We assert the vision of community, tolerance, compassion, justice, and the sacredness of human life, which lies at the heart of all our religious traditions. America must be a safe place for all our citizens in all their diversity. It is especially important that our citizens who share national origins, ethnicity, or religion with whoever attacked us are, themselves, protected among us.

Our American illusion of invulnerability has been shattered. From now on, we will look at the world in a different way, and this attack on our life as a nation will become a test of our national character. Let us make the right choices in this crisis—to pray, act, and unite against the bitter fruits of division, hatred, and violence. Let us rededicate ourselves to global peace, human dignity, and the eradication of injustice that breeds rage and vengeance.

As we gather in our houses of worship, let us begin a process of seeking the healing and grace of God.

Reprinted with permission from the National Council of Churches <www.ncccusa.org>.

General Synod Speaks on Terrorism, War, a Just Peace, and Active Peacemaking

❀

JUSTICE AND WITNESS MINISTRIES
UNITED CHURCH OF CHRIST

*Neither terrorists nor those responding to terrorism can afford
to demonize and dehumanize persons or nations.*

GENERAL SYNOD MEETS EVERY TWO YEARS, and one of the important tasks of delegates is to provide guidance to local congregations and the national settings of the church on important issues. General Synods have repeatedly spoken to issues of war and violence and have consistently called for active peacemaking work by all parts of the United Church of Christ, whatever the threat or concern. This document summarizes such guidance with an eye to the concerns posed by the attacks of September 11, 2001, and the following bio-terrorist attacks.

The world has changed for all of us since September 11. From 1971, and even earlier, General Synods have focused a great deal of attention on opposing the brutal effects on poor nations of various foreign policies, military and related activities, and economic policies of the United States. Now the United States has suffered terrorist attacks and, though General Synod statements did not anticipate this situation, their words are highly relevant for our efforts to respond.

TERRORISM

In the priority statement "Peace and U.S. Power," the Eighth General Synod in 1971 challenged the churches "to develop understanding and support indigenous liberation movements which oppose elitist oppression or totalitarian subversion." The United Church of Christ has supported many indigenous liberation movements, at home and abroad. Osama bin Laden claims that the al-Qu'aida is such an indigenous liberation movement. The Northern Alliance in Afghanistan claims that it is opposing elitist oppression when it fights against the Taliban and bin Laden. Regardless of who feels just cause in a conflict, General Synods have repeatedly opposed war as a means for settling disputes.

The Eighth General Synod forcefully condemned the indiscriminate killing of civilians and military personnel through chemical and biological warfare. The Seventeenth General Synod in 1989 condemned terrorism in the resolution "U.S. Overt and Covert Military Intervention," noting that "brutalization and terrorization of civilians is a regular feature of covert warfare." In the pronouncement "Affirming the United Church of Christ as a Just Peace Church," passed by the Fifteenth General Synod in 1985, the United Church of Christ rejects "the labeling of others as enemies and the creation of institutions which perpetuate enemy relations." Neither terrorists nor those responding to terrorism can afford to demonize and dehumanize persons or nations.

General Synod offers the most direct guidance for opposing terrorism when it declared "our opposition to war, violence, and terrorism" and the Fifteenth General Synod called all nations to declare that they will not attack another nation. *Terrorism, however great one's cause may seem to be, has been consistently opposed by General Synods.* The "war without boundaries," as well as specific means of terrorism, has usually been addressed in the context of other nations but the right to protection against terrorism certainly applies to the United States as well.

THE UNITED STATES WAR ON TERRORISM

The statement of the Seventeenth General Synod, "U.S. Overt and Covert Military Intervention," was born out of a concern about the involvement of the United States in several clandestine and open wars in Central America and other parts of the world in the 1970s and 1980s. The synod declared that "covert operations and covert war violate both international law and basic democratic principles." Since the Second and Third General Synods in 1959 and 1961, there has been repeated affirmation of the critical role of international institutions in mediating conflicts, such as U.N. peacekeeping operations. Insofar as the current U.S. war on terrorism is not in accord with international law and employs overt and covert actions in undeclared wars, reaching potentially into any nation that harbors terrorism (including our own), it would fail United Church of Christ policy as created by General Synods. For example, food drops and sanctions, in the context of military activity, are forbidden by the Geneva Convention rules governing the conduct of war.

The Eighth General Synod in 1971 lifted concerns about the infringement of human rights by governments in pursuit of peace. This would challenge the antiterrorism legislation recently passed by Congress, which significantly expands the ability of the U.S. government to monitor the free movement of U.S. citizens. The Tenth General Synod in 1975 explicitly states concerns about the expansion of covert activity of the CIA in times of war and repressive activity by the federal government against people in the United States.

A JUST PEACE

The Fifteenth General Synod in 1985 established the most comprehensive policy on war and peace for the United Church of Christ in the pronouncement "Affirming the United Church of Christ as a Just Peace Church." One aspect of that guidance is that governments have the right and obligation "to use civil authority to prevent lawlessness and protect human rights." But the right to self-defense is not an unconstrained right, according to the Fifteenth General Synod. It questions the actions of governments that engage in the excessive protections, particularly if such protective acts do not have the primary mission of "creating social justice and promoting human welfare." *In short, the Fifteenth General Synod recognized the right to self-defense within the lament that we live*

in a world where war is seen as the primary instrument of national policy instead of global,
racial, social, or economic justice.

The Eighth General Synod supported the right of young persons to file for Conscientious Objection to military draft, calling on the UCC to "develop vigorous ministries to insure that each youth who faces the draft will have access to competent draft counseling." The Eighth General Synod also directs us to "develop ministries designed to minister to individuals and families who are caught in the agony of participating in wars as well as to those individuals and families who object to wars." The Eighth General Synod and many others call for a negotiated peace between Israel and Palestine.

The guidance is clear that the United Church of Christ must continue to balance concerns for justice for all with the concern of freedom from violence for all. This is a tension at the heart of the phrase "a Just Peace church" and at the heart of earlier Christian doctrines concerning war—pacifism, just war, and crusade. Active peacemaking, one constant in every General Synod statement concerning war and violence, has been to emphasize that Christian action must be guided by a Christian concern to actively promote peace. The UCC is repeatedly challenged to not be merely responsive to the circumstances as defined by other governments, or our own government, but to actively pursue the "things that make for peace." As the Fifteenth General Synod put it, although "*evil and violence are imbedded in human nature and institutions, [and] will remain present in some form . . . war can and must be eliminated.*"

In the proposal for action that went along with the Just Peace Church pronouncement, numerous suggestions for active peacemaking were presented. Further development of peacemaking strategies and activities are available in the book *A Just Peace Church* and a more recent book, *Just Peacemaking*, both available from The Pilgrim Press. Additional resource materials from all the Covenanted Ministries of the UCC have been posted on the UCC Web page <www.ucc.org> and are also available from the Public Life and Social Policy Team; Justice and Witness Ministries; United Church of Christ; 110 Maryland Avenue NE, #207; Washington, D.C. 20002; phone 202.543.1517.

Reprinted by permission. From a Justice and Witness Ministries-produced bulletin insert, October 2001.

Reflections on the Events of September 11

❈

SCOTT SIMON

ON SEPTEMBER 25, 2001, Proclamation, Identity, and Communication sponsored the Nineteenth Annual Parker Lecture. Scott Simon, host of National Public Radio's Weekend Edition, was the keynote speaker. Simon spent many hours covering the terrorist strike at the World Trade Center. We asked him to share his reflections. This is what he had to say.

I am grateful for the opportunity to speak with you at what is so clearly an urgent time. With your permission, I will depart from the line of remarks I had initially sketched out and address myself explicitly to these times.

I can certainly be expansive on the subject of broadcasting and how we are—or are not—meeting our responsibilities. But those observations would now be small-minded. The fact is, during the recent weeks of crisis, all major broadcasters—not only including but specifically much-maligned commercial broadcasters—have met those responsibilities with professionalism and devotion. This week, they have only my admiration.

I suspect that what I have to say today about war and peace will not please a good many of you. I don't want you to feel compelled to offer courteous applause for remarks with which you may vigorously disagree. I am grateful for the chance just to be heard in this forum; that is as much courtesy as I can expect. So let me suggest that my remarks be received simply with silence.

There is nothing good to be said about tragedy or terror. But miseries can distill a sense of utter clarity—remind us of who we are; whom we love; and what is worth giving our lives for.

When Jeremy Glick of Hewitt, New Jersey, called his wife Lyzbeth during the last moments of United Flight 93 he said:

"I love you. Don't be sad. Take care of our daughter. Whatever you do is okay with me."

The depth of his love compressed and clear as a diamond.

Over the past ten days, the pain of loss and fear of terror may have caused many Americans to admit to themselves how much they really love their country. Love it not blindly but with unblinking awareness.

They love that frivolous America that proclaims pride in 31 flavors of ice cream—but also the solemn mission of having a gaudy Times Square assortment of all the world's peoples within its borders.

They love the America that can be shallow, giddy, and greedy—but also funny, delightful, and generous.

America can abound with silly, malicious, and even dangerous ideas—because people here are free to express any damn-fool idea that comes to them.

America can be bigoted and inhospitable—but it also takes strangers from all over the world into its arms.

America has now been targeted by a few blind souls who are willing to kill thousands—and themselves—to make this nation bleed. But far more people from around the world have already been willing to die—over-packed into holds of ships and trucks—just to have a small chance to live here.

It's not that Americans don't want their country to change, in a thousand ways, from making good medical care available to all Americans to abolishing the designated-hitter rule. But the blast at our emblems last week has made many Americans see their nation as that place in the world where change is still most possible.

Patriotism has often been the last refuge of scoundrels—and we've had those scoundrels. But what hiding place is open to those who twist their faith into a weapon to run through innocent people?

Do we really want to live in the kind of world such blind souls would make for us? In the end, the choice may be that harsh: to live in a world that revolves around fear—or in America, with all its faults?

Now I say this knowing that we have our own American mullahs, and by this I don't mean—in fact, I specifically do not mean—American Muslims who have recently been the object of harassment. I am not of a mind to be obscure about this: I mean specifically the Reverends Jerry Falwell and Pat Robertson. Please permit me to repeat the thrust of some remarks I delivered this past weekend. In a way, I am grateful for this duo: They renewed my capacity to be shocked at a time I thought my sense of shock had been exhausted.

Right after the terrorist strikes in New York and here in Washington, when America was wounded and confused, the Reverend Falwell was a guest on Pat Robertson's 700 Club. He said that God Almighty, angered by America's abortion rights, gay rights, and secularism in the schools, had permitted terrorists to slay the World Trade Center and smite the Pentagon:

"What we saw on Tuesday," said Mr. Falwell, "could be minuscule if in fact God continues to lift the curtain and allow the enemies of America to give us probably what we deserve."

Mr. Robertson joined in, saying, "Jerry, that's my feeling. I think we've just seen the antechamber to terror. We haven't even begun to see what they can do to the major population."

Then Mr. Falwell concluded, "I really believe that the pagans, and the abortionists, and the feminists, and the gays and lesbians who are actively trying to make that an alternative lifestyle, the ACLU, People for the American Way—all of them who have tried to secularize America—I point the finger in their face and say, you helped this happen."

Last week, both the reverends issued apologies. Mr. Falwell called his own remarks, "insensitive, uncalled for, and unnecessary"—everything but wrong.

Also last week, it was reported that Mark Bingham, a San Francisco public-relations executive, may well have been one of the passengers who so bravely resisted the hijackers of United Airlines Flight 93, which crashed into an unpopulated field instead of another national monument.

Mr. Bingham was thirty-one. He played on a local gay rugby team and hoped to compete in next year's Gay Games in Sydney, Australia.

I don't know if Mark Bingham was religious. But it seems to me that he lived a life that celebrated the preciousness of this world's infinite variety—while the Reverends Robertson and Falwell and the mullahs of the Taliban see a God who smiles with approval on murder and destruction.

Let me put it in the bald terms in which many Americans may be thinking right now: If your plane was hijacked, who would you rather sit next to? Righteous reverends who will sit back and say, "This is God's punishment for gay Teletubbies?" Or the gay rugby player who lays down his life to save others?

And by the way: which person seems closer to God?

One of the unforeseen effects of being in journalism is that your first-hand exposure to the issues of the world sometimes has the consequence of shaking your deepest personal convictions. I happen to be a Quaker; this is known; I have written about this, especially in my memoir, *Home and Away*, which, if you would please permit a small parochial note here, is now available in paperback. I covered conflicts in Central America and the Caribbean, the Middle East and Africa. None of them shook my belief that pacifism offers the world a way to foment change without the violence that has pained and poisoned our history.

Gandhi and Nehru's nonviolent revolution gave India a skilled and sturdy democracy rather than another violent religious tyranny. Nelson Mandela's willingness to employ deliberate and peaceful protest against the brutalities of apartheid made today's South Africa an inspiration to the world of the power of reconciliation and hope. Martin Luther King's campaign to bring down American segregation; Corazon Aquino's People Power revolution in the Philippines; pacifism has had its heroes, its martyrs, its losses, and its victories.

My pacifism was not absolute. About half the draft-age Quakers and Mennonites in North America enlisted during World War II on the idea that whatever solutions non-violence had to offer the world, it was without a response to Adolph Hitler. I hope I would have been among those who enlisted.

And then, in the 1990s, I covered the Balkans. And I had to confront, in flesh and blood, the real life flaw—I am inclined to say literally fatal flaw—of pacifism: all the best people could be killed by all the worst ones. Bosnia, we might remind ourselves, had the ambition of being the Costa Rica of the Balkans, an unarmed democracy that would shine out to the world. Its surrounding adversaries were not impressed or deterred by this aspiration.

Slobodan Milosovic will now stand trial before the world—but only after a quarter of a million people in Bosnia and Kosovo have been killed. Forgive me if I do not count his delivery for trial as a victory for international law and, therefore, a model to now be emulated. In fact, I am appalled by the fact that much of the evidence presented against him at trial will almost undoubtedly be derived from U.S. intelligence information. That evidence will be used to try to convict Milosovic after he has committed murder because America lacked the will to use its military might to prevent those killings. I doubt that future despots will be much deterred by this example.

So I speak as a Quaker of not particularly good standing. I am still willing to give first consideration to peaceful alternatives. But I am not willing to lose lives for the sake of ideological consistency. As Mahatma Gandhi himself once said, and, like Lincoln, the Mahatma is wonderful for providing quotations that permit you to prove almost any point you choose, "I would rather be inconsistent than wrong."

It seems to me that in confronting the forces that attacked the World Trade Center and the Pentagon, the United States has no sane alternative but to wage war and wage it with unflinching resolution.

Notice I don't say reprisal or revenge. What I mean is self-defense—protecting the United States from further attack by destroying those who would launch them.

There is a certain quarter of opinion in the United States—we certainly hear from them at NPR—who, perhaps still in shock, seem to believe that the attacks against New York and Washington were natural disasters: horrible, spontaneous whirlwinds that struck once and will not reoccur.

This is wrong. It is even inexcusably foolish. The United States has been targeted for destruction. We know now that more hijackings were likely planned for September 11. Other agents were at least exploring the possibilities of other kinds of attacks, including sending crop-dusters over cities with poisonous chemicals. If you dismissed these kinds of scenarios as Hollywood folderol before, it is just not informed to do so now. There is an ongoing violent campaign aimed at bringing down the United States. How many more skyscrapers and national monuments—and the people in them—how many more citizens are we willing to lose?

There are some quarters of world opinion that believe that simply delivering those who plotted the attack to international justice should suffice. But this is not the nature of the danger we confront—literally, physically, in this very city—which is present, persistent, and current. Simply arresting those who executed the attacks in New York and Washington will not deter other assaults that we must assume are proceeding right now.

There are some quarters of opinion that say, just this bluntly, that Americans somehow invited this attack down upon ourselves—that this attack was some kind of recompense for holding slaves a century and a half ago, for extinguishing native tribes from America, for interning Japanese-Americans during a world war sixty years ago, for overthrowing Salvador Allende in Chile, or for standing by Israel, however the Mossad behaves.

None of those individual assertions are untrue. All of them irrelevant.

The people who make these arguments usually consider themselves at the polar opposite of Falwell and Robertson. But are they? They say that those who died in New York and Washington have only their country to blame for their deaths. By ignoring the extensive advancement America has made towards becoming a just society, they make it seem as though sins that are centuries and decades old can never be overcome by progress.

Some very fine minds have become so skilled at playing this parlor game of moral relativism that they make little in American life seem worthwhile. They insist, in so many ways, that the United States cannot criticize the Taliban for enslaving women in the twenty-first century because some of New York police practiced racial profiling; that the United States does not have the moral standing to oppose terrorism, because we once supported the Shah of Iran.

This kind of rhetorical exchange can go on endlessly—and it shouldn't. Sharp and powerful minds should be applied to something more productive right now.

How would those who now urge reconciliation accomplish that? Reconcile ourselves to what? Should we surrender Manhattan Island? Iowa, Utah, or Hollywood? Should we impose a unitary religious state on these shores, throw American women out of school and work, and rob all other religious groups of any rights so that we will have the kind of society that our attackers will accept? Should we renounce our pledge to make a home for those we turned away from our shores during the Holocaust and abandon Israel?

To reconcile ourselves in any way with the blind souls who flew against New York and Washington and who have other targets within their sights now is to hand our own lives over into wickedness.

I'm glad to see reporting now that asks, "Why do they hate us?" We need to hear the complaints of those who experience U.S. foreign policy, sometimes at the blunt end. But I would not want our increasing erudition to distract us from the answer that applies to those who are now physically attacking the United States: They hate us because they are psychotics. They should be taken no more seriously as political theorists than Charles Manson or Timothy McVeigh.

There are also a number of Americans—and we hear from them—who suggest that this war should not be fought because a number of Americans who are Muslims have been the objects of threats and harassment. Those attacks against Muslims are reprehensible. Every American of every stripe has the obligation to disown and prevent them.

I have been impressed by President Bush's determination to make the rights of Muslim Americans and American respect for Muslim nations an essential part of U.S. policy. This is vastly different from the actions that were inflicted against Japanese-Americans during World War II. The difference between the damage that good liberals of their time, Earl Warren, Franklin Roosevelt, and Hugo Black, imposed on an ethnic minority in 1941 and what conservatives of this time, George W. Bush, Rudolph Giuliani, and John Ashcroft, have specifically avoided doing radiantly represents America's ability to improve itself.

Over the past ten years, every time the United States has committed itself to a military deployment, explicitly in the Gulf War, then in Somalia, and over the skies of

Bosnia and Kosovo, it has been in the defense of Muslim peoples. At the same time, tens of thousands of Muslim students and other immigrants have been accepted into the United States. American Muslims now number close to six million.

We still suffer the stain of racial and ethnic bigotry. But this largely peaceful incorporation of Islam into American life should be a source of pride that is not belittled by the actions of a few cranks and bigots. Surely we have the means to defeat them, too.

I can conjure a score of reasons why this war should not be fought. The terrorists who struck are ruthless and undaunted even by their own deaths. The war will kill some, perhaps many, of our own best people; the first attack already has—the firefighters and police who perished in the World Trade Center. The war will be lengthy and costly, and it may be impossible to tell when it is done. There will be no unequivocal surrender. And just when we may begin to feel a sense of safety returning, another strike may occur. The war may restrict some of our traditional liberties to travel, unfettered, across our own nation.

And yet, to back away from this war would be to accept all of that as permanent. To live the rest of our lives, not just a few years, with deaths delivered by people dying by terrorist bombs, chemical attacks, and the successive devices of sharp and ruthless minds; to live out our futures with our liberties shrinking as our losses and fears expand.

I do not accept that this war must cost us our best qualities. American men and women often wreaked terrible punishments on their adversaries in Germany and Japan, from the fire bombing of Dresden to the incineration of Hiroshima, and, by the way, that kind of retaliatory brutality is in no way justifiable or necessary in the conflict at hand now. Those men and women returned to their families and proceeded to pay their own tax dollars into those programs that rebuilt the nations they fought so fiercely and fermented the civil rights movement at home.

Yes, there was the blight of McCarthyite witch hunts, the prolonged and pernicious mistake of the war in Vietnam, and CIA incursions into Nicaragua, Iran, and God-knows-where else.

But do we genuinely believe that we would live in a better world today if the West had used its own flaws and sins as a moral license to avoid fighting world fascism? Would Martin Luther King have succeeded in changing our world so palpably if his opponent had been Adolph Hitler instead of an overstuffed Bull Connor, opposed by the U.S. Federal government?

None of us are immaculate and innocent past the age of six. But we cannot avoid making judgments—sometimes harsh ones—for the rest of our lives. One of those judgments is upon us now.

I think that peace activists can sometimes commit the same error in judgment as generals: They prepare to fight the last war not the next one. The conflict before us now does not involve American power intruding in places where it has interests but American power intervening to save lives where only American power can be effective.

We are living in a time when we must remind ourselves of the imperfections of analogies. But let me press ahead with one that has recently been on my mind.

In 1933, the Oxford Student Union conducted a famous debate over whether it was moral for Britons to fight for king and country. The leading objective minds of that university reviewed the many ways in which British colonialism exploited and oppressed the world. They cited the ways in which vengeful demands made of Germany in the wake of the end of World War I had helped encourage the kind of nationalism that may have kindled the rise of fascism. They saw no moral difference between western colonialism and world fascism. The Oxford Union ended that debate with this famous proclamation: "Resolved, that we will in no circumstances fight for king and country."

Von Ribbentrop sent back the good news to Germany's new chancellor, Adolph Hitler: The West will not fight for its own survival. Its finest minds will justify a silent surrender.

The most intelligent young people of their time could not tell the difference between the deficiencies of their own nation, in which liberty and democracy occupied cornerstones, and dictatorship founded on racism, tyranny, and fear.

But Mahatma Gandhi knew the difference. He spent World War II in a prison in Poona and sat on his hands and spun cloth, rather than to raise a hand in revolt against England when it was most vulnerable. He knew that, in the end, a world that was spun by German and Japanese Fascism offered no hope to the oppressed of this planet. And, in fact, at the close of World War II, Britain divested itself of empire: exhausted by its own defense, to be sure, but also ennobled by defending its own best ideals.

Have thoughtful, moral Americans in the twenty-first century become so exquisitely sensitive to the sins and shortcomings of the United States, so comfortable with the lack of resolution that moral relativism promotes, that we do not see the blessing that it has been put into our hands to protect—an incomparably diverse and democratic nation?

When George Orwell returned to England after fighting against fascism in the Spanish civil war, he felt uneasy over finding his country so comfortable—so close to fascism. His country, he said, with its fat Sunday newspapers and thick orange jam.

"All sleeping the deep, deep sleep," he wrote, "from which I sometimes fear that we shall never wake till we are jerked out of it by the roar of bombs."

Delivered September 25, 2001, at the Nineteenth Annual Parker Lecture at National City Christian Church, Washington, D.C. Reprinted by permission.

My Christmas Prayer

❀

BERNICE POWELL JACKSON

EVERY YEAR for the past three or four years, I've had the very same Christmas wish. This year, with all that's happened over the past twelve months, maybe it needs to be more than a wish—it needs to be a prayer. It is simply a prayer for peace.

Last December, I was in Bethlehem, the famous little town of Jesus' birth. Last December, the Israeli Defense Forces had shut it down during the second Intifada. This year, only a few weeks ago, Israeli army tanks rolled through the streets and U.S. attack helicopters were shelling homes in Beit Jala, a mostly Christian community only a mile or so away from Bethlehem. This year, not only is there no peace in Bethlehem, there is no peace in Jerusalem or in any part of the Gaza strip. More than 1,000 Palestinians and Israelis have died in the past fifteen months, many of them children and young people. Suicide bombers have increased, as have the assassinations of those deemed terrorists by Israeli forces. Innocents die on both sides. My fervent prayer is for an end to the downward spiral of violence whose vortex threatens to pull us all into war.

Of course, any prayer for peace in 2001 must include a prayer for an end to the horror of terrorism. With the deaths of more than 3,000 Americans in the September 11 terrorist attacks, Americans are aware in a new and personal way of the devastation that can be caused by a few filled with hate or who feel there is no other way to take control of their lives. Tragically, many around the world have suffered that kind of terrorism and that kind of fear for years. My prayer is for an end to the violence of terrorism and a prayer that, somehow, those families who have lost loved ones in the attacks this year will find some measure of peace.

But as millions of people around the world yearn for peace in their nations, millions also yearn for peace in their communities. While the gang violence of the 1990s seems to have peaked, there are still children dying in drive-by shootings in cities across the land. And if police had not been informed and had not intervened in western Massachusetts only weeks ago, there would have been another Columbine-type shooting of high school students and teachers. Too much violence in our communities, too many young people in the inner cities and in the suburbs are turning to guns as the answer to their pain and frustration. My prayer is for peace in the 'hood and peace in communities around the world.

Only a few weeks ago in Cleveland, where I live, a thirteen-year-old boy was convicted and sentenced for murdering his father. That child was a victim of domestic violence and abuse for his entire life. His was a story of both abuse and abandonment. He was abandoned by his mother, who fled to save her own life but left her son behind to live in an abusive environment. Abandoned by relatives who knew of the abuse but turned a blind eye. Abandoned by the schools, which did on several occasions report the father but did not continue to follow through. Abandoned by the state, which knew of the abuse and yet did not offer the child the protection he so needed. Abandoned now by the criminal justice system and a judge who said that she would consider psychological treatment for the boy if he "behaved" while he is in detention. This child's story is only one story of a victim of violence in the home. My prayer is that all those who cannot find peace, even in their homes, will find peace this Christmas and may those of us who know about their abuse find ways to help them this holiday season.

The world cries out for peace. My prayer is simply a prayer for peace. May it be so.

Reprinted by permission. From the syndicated column "Witness for Justice" (December 2001), a column published for more than twenty years that engages critical issues of our day and is written to educate both church and society, to stimulate conversation, and to call us to action.

Justice and Witness Ministries Board Statement

October 28, 2001

❀

JUSTICE AND WITNESS MINISTRIES BOARD
UNITED CHURCH OF CHRIST

DEAR SISTERS AND BROTHERS IN CHRIST,

Greetings and peace in the name of Jesus Christ, the Prince of Peace!

We write this letter to you as members of the Board of Directors of Justice and Witness Ministries and as members of many local churches of the United Church of Christ, seeking to find courage in the struggle for justice and peace in today's world. We write because of our commitment to "making things right" and to restoring peace with justice in our nation and in the world.

As individuals and Christians who care deeply about our country and its people and who grieve for the loss of so many lives, we struggle to comprehend and faithfully respond to the shock and tragedy of September 11 as well as to the military retaliation against Afghanistan. We know that these are not easy times for all people of faith as we struggle to determine what is the moral course for our nation. We acknowledge that many of our sisters and brothers in Christ support our government's relentless bombing of Afghanistan. But we are called to offer a word of peace in a time of war and we are called to express our patriotism through our faithfulness and to what we know about biblical justice. We believe that God calls us to be peacemakers, healers, and the "repairers of the breach" of which the prophet Isaiah speaks (Is.: 58:12).

We offer you this letter as one way to encourage our churches to engage in thoughtful discussion about the very complex realities facing our world and to urge responses that affirm our belief that there can be no peace without justice. As we discussed with each other the terrorist attacks and the onset of war, we found ourselves searching the living word contained in the teachings of Jesus and the prophets, and in more contemporary General Synod actions such as the "Just Peace Church Pronouncement," adopted in 1985, and the resolution passed this past summer that calls on the United Church of Christ in all its settings to support and participate in the World Council of Churches' "Decade to Overcome Violence." We commend these words of our church to you as well.

We also received the testimony and witness of United Church of Christ members, including youth and young adults, who were delegates to the World Conference on Racism, Intolerance, Xenophobia, and Related Forms of Discrimination that met in Durban, South Africa, two weeks before September 11. They reminded us that we are part of a global community in which many people experience the policies of the government of the United States of America as oppressive and directly contributing to their misery. While our nation has prospered, too many people in the world have suffered.

Too many know unending hunger and thirst, chronic unemployment, homelessness, illness, and early death.

How, then, do we, as Justice and Witness Ministries, charged with a mandate for prophetic witness, respond to what is happening in the world where:

- Hundreds of hate crimes have been perpetrated against Muslims, persons perceived to be of Middle Eastern descent and others.

- More than one thousand persons of the Islamic faith or Middle Eastern decent are being held in U.S. jails without due process of law.

- Racial profiling is once again on the rise as suspicion and fear grip our nation and is excused by many because of the crisis.

- "The war on terrorism" is being used to justify a rushed legislative agenda in Congress, some of which is irrelevant to the crisis and that includes, for example, fast track authority on trade treaties, authorization for oil drilling in the Arctic National Wilderness Area, expansion of Plan Colombia and other foreign military investments, promotion of the National Missile Defense System, and tax cuts that ignore the needs of the poor.

- Unrestrained federal spending since September 11, focused on military retaliation and anti-terrorism measures, threatens to further weaken economic protection for the poor and elderly, including prescription drug relief for the elderly, Temporary Assistance to Needy Families, Social Security benefits, health care, and other programs.

- Low-wage workers, especially immigrants, are losing their jobs by the thousands every day in industries impacted by the war and the global economic recession.

- Serious compromises to our civil liberties have already been approved in the Anti-Terrorism Act passed by Congress.

We believe peace is not merely the absence of war but the presence of just social relations. We believe that God calls us to work for this shalom for all human beings, who were created in God's own image. For us, this means that God's love extends to everyone, not just to citizens of the United States or to Christians. We believe that we are called to follow Christ's commandments to love and forgive, and we are challenged by Jesus' words to love our enemies and pray for those who persecute us (Mt. 5:43–48).

We are grateful to those among us who have spoken out boldly, based on our call to be a Just Peace church and understand that our church must stand up for the justice and peace expressed by the one who is our foundation—Jesus Christ. We invite other members of the United Church of Christ and our partners in other denominations and faith traditions to join us in seeking to read the signs of the times and to discern what God is calling us to say and to do in these difficult days.

We recommit ourselves to being repairers of the breach. Recalling Jesus' words of encouragement that "blessed are the peacemakers," we invite you to intensify your peacemaking efforts and to join us in the process of making things right again. Whether that is making a situation right within your family, making things right in your community or making things right by joining in private prayer or public witness to help call the soul of this nation back toward peace and constructive dialogue and away from violence and vengeance, we ask you to join us.

Together, let us work for that beloved community, bound together by God's shalom for God's creation, so that our children and our children's children may know a world of justice and a world of peace.

This statement was approved by the Board of Directors of the United Church of Christ's Justice and Witness Ministries on Sunday, October 28, during a regular meeting held in Cleveland, Ohio. There was one dissent. Some members of the board were not able to be in attendance.

Make Us Instruments of Your Peace

A Pastoral Letter of the Covenanted Ministries
of the United Church of Christ

❀

JOINT STATEMENT OF THE COVENANTED BOARDS

APRIL 21, 2002

Lord, make me an instrument of your peace. Where there is hatred, let me sow love; where there is injury, pardon; where there is doubt, faith; where there is despair, hope; where there is darkness, light; where there is sadness, joy . . .

We, the members of the boards of the Covenanted Ministries of the United Church of Christ, meeting jointly April 18–21, 2002, in St. Louis, Missouri, greet you in the name of our risen Savior Jesus Christ. During this time, when the world cries out amid violence, we extend to you our deepest appreciation that in the wake of the tragedies of September 11, 2001, our church has chosen the way of peace.

In our ministry with people most directly affected by those events, including our own members and their families, our churches have contributed over $2 million for immediate and long-term assistance through One Great Hour of Sharing's special disaster appeal, "Hope from the Rubble." Roughly three-quarters of that amount has enabled a coordinated response through Church World Service and local ecumenical and interfaith organizations, as well as local United Church of Christ efforts, to provide skilled counseling to people throughout the region, offering support for pastors and lay people alike, including a special outreach to children. Five hundred thousand dollars has been designated to address the long-term effects of toxic materials and health-related issues at Ground Zero in New York City.

We want to thank you, as well, for the many additional ways you have given and continue to give of yourselves in the months since the tragedy: our pastors' spiritual care and counsel; lay persons volunteering their time and skills, donating blood or tending to frightened children; many extending the hand of generosity once again by sending contributions to our special appeal to assist those suffering in Afghanistan. This generosity is a testimony to our church's choice to affirm life in the face of the cruelty and barbarism of the September 11 attacks and the subsequent bombing and loss of life in Afghanistan.

The events of September 11 shook us at our very foundations. They shattered our illusions of security. Many among us began to seek security through the abrogation of the rights that we have proudly claimed to be the hallmark of a democratic society. For example, the U.S.A. Patriot Act, signed into law on October 26, 2001, gives virtually unchecked power to the executive branch of our government. It imposes new limitations on our freedoms of speech and association; it permits, without judicial approval, surveillance of political activists and organizations deemed to oppose U.S. policies; it circumvents the Fourth Amendment in permitting government monitoring of the Internet, e-mail, and even private telephone conversations; it permits mandatory detention, without trial, of non-citizens in our midst, including those held at the U.S. military base at Guantanamo Bay, Cuba.

Our church has a history of critiquing the "conventional wisdom" of the day. We have opposed slavery, tyranny, and discrimination against those who were considered "different" or "suspect." This heritage, based in our commitment to life in Christ, calls us to oppose such measures in our own society and to offer an alternative view of where our security lies—in belonging to and living for Christ through the advocacy and safe-guarding of justice and in extending the hand of hospitality to those deemed "foreign."

We choose the way of peace for the people of Afghanistan, who have seen too much death and devastation from war, oppressive governments, and natural disasters. We abhor the Taliban's disregard for human rights. We earnestly hope and pray that the new provisional government of Afghanistan will be able to transcend the dubious pasts of many of the participants in that new government. At the same time, we question whether war can truly eradicate the root causes of terrorism, and we lament the proposed military expenditures to sustain such a war and the temptation to restore a first-strike nuclear policy. Afghanistan needs to be built up, not further destroyed. Our nation's resources should be used to bring the hope of new life, not the continuing prospect of death for the innocent and the unknown.

We are told by U.S. policy-makers that military action against Iraq is necessary in the quest for security. This course of action, in addition to being immensely unpopular among our Arab and European allies, flies in the face of recent experience. United States military action against Saddam Hussein and the imposition of strict economic sanctions against Iraq have only strengthened his tyrannical regime while bringing untold misery to the Iraqi people. As Christians called to feed the hungry and clothe the naked, we reiterate our call for the removal of sanctions against Iraq, which have only victimized the most vulnerable, and our call for the avoidance of military action, which in the past has only solidified Saddam Hussein's hold on power and enhanced his popularity in the Arab world.

The resolution of the Arab–Israeli–Palestinian conflict remains the key to regional and international stability. The United States, because of its special relationships in the area, bears unique responsibility for helping to achieve peace. Israelis and Palestinians—Jews, Christians, and Muslims—have suffered far too long, and now live in constant fear of each other. A state of war prevails, featuring, on the one hand, the random and senseless violence of suicide bombers and, on the other, the "reoccupation" of Palestinian lands, with attacks by tanks and aircraft, checkpoints and curfews, assaults and demolitions of homes and orchards, and the imprisonment and public humiliation of Palestinian leadership.

Again, we are called to choose the way of peace. We condemn the violence used by all parties to the conflict, even as we recognize the imbalance in capacity that favors

Israel. As in the past, we affirm the right of Israel to secure borders and peace with its neighbors, but we also insist on the rights of the Palestinian people to sovereignty and self-determination. Placing the phenomenon of suicide bombers within the context of the "war on terrorism" cloaks the reality of injustice that provokes some to such desperate and self-destructive acts. Similarly, criticism of the policies of the government of Israel should not give excuse for the latent—and sometimes overt—anti-Semitism that has been such a scourge in the past and that is experiencing renewal in Europe and in the United States. We honor our kindred relationship with Jews and Muslims, siblings within the Abrahamic tradition.

We support efforts to bring peace with justice to the Holy Land and yearn for the day when the prayers of all believers will mingle together in Jerusalem in a symphony of peace. To this end, we pledge to continue to pray and engage our nation's policy, and we join the international ecumenical community in supporting the World Council of Churches' Decade to Overcome Violence and especially its initial focus on Israel and Palestine. We affirm and pledge our cooperation in the Council's initiative to implement an ecumenical accompaniment program in both Palestine and Israel as a promising strategy to thwart the escalation of violence. Our witness shall be our accompaniment of both Israelis and Palestinians as they seek a way out of the current deadly cycle of death and destruction.

In the wake of September 11, we choose the way of peace, having experienced the horror of terror and death. We would resist the temptation to solve the world's problems by the use of the implements of war. In a world in which the United States functions as sole superpower, we in the church are called to witness to the interdependence of all people and that, in God's eyes, the life of every human being is precious. We would be Christ's body in this world, loving all of our neighbors, even resisting the powers and principalities to demonstrate in our lives that we are followers of Christ's Way.

> For it is in giving that we receive; it is in pardoning that we are pardoned; and it is in dying that we are born to eternal life. —*Saint Francis of Assisi, 1181(?)–1226*

This pastoral letter was approved Sunday, April 21, 2002, by a vote of each of the boards of directors of the Covenanted Ministries of the United Church of Christ: Justice and Witness Ministries, Local Church Ministries, the Office of General Ministries, and Wider Church Ministries. These four bodies conduct U.S. and global ministries on behalf of the 1.3-million-member United Church of Christ, which has nearly 6,000 local churches in the United States and Puerto Rico. The four boards of directors consist of a total of 229 laypersons and ordained ministers from throughout the church. The document was also "affirmed" on Tuesday, April 23, 2002, by vote of the 76-member Executive Council of the United Church of Christ, which conducts denominational business between the biennial meetings of the church's General Synod. This pastoral letter, intended for church-wide and public distribution, speaks to (and not for) the members and local churches of the United Church of Christ.

SEND US, O GOD
A Prayer of Commitment

~

When those who were around him saw
what was coming, they asked, "Lord, should we
strike with the sword?" Then one of them struck the
slave of the high priest and cut off his right ear.
But Jesus said, "No more of this!"

—Luke 22:49–51

Then I heard the voice of the Lord saying,
"Whom shall I send, and who will go for us?"
And I said, "Here I am, send me!"

—Isaiah 6:8

~

A Prayer of Commitment after September 11

May, 2002

❀

ELIZABETH C. NORDBECK

THE PSALMIST SAYS:
The earth is the Lord's and the fullness thereof.
    The world, and all that dwell in it.
But who will ascend the hill of the Lord?
And who will stand in God's holy places?

Who will go down to the cities—
    Where blood is poured out like water on the mean streets,
    Where despair begets brutality, and frustration, fear;
        And lives are daily offered up on the altars of anger and hatred?
Who will go down to the cities, and speak a word of hope?
We are yours, O God; send us.

The earth is the Lord's and the fullness thereof.
But who will go up to the mountains—
    Where the smoke from burning forests draws a shroud over places that were green,
    Where the careless habitations of humanity stretch off to the horizon,
        And grey mist rises everywhere to meet blue sky?
Who will go up to the mountains, and speak a word of warning?
We are yours, O God; send us.

The earth is the Lord's and the fullness thereof.
But who will go into the homes—
    Where young bodies and old lie pained and dying,
    Where spirits crushed and broken seek the false solace of solitude,
        And hidden lives pass desperate days behind closed doors?
Who will go into the homes, and speak a word of healing?
We are yours, O God; send us.

The earth is the Lord's and the fullness thereof.
But who will go out to the public square—
    Where words do not mean what they seem to say,
    Where speeches are spun, not spoken,
        And honesty is a synonym for foolishness?
Who will go out to the public square, and speak a word of truth?
We are yours, O God; send us.

We *are* yours, O God. Send us forth boldly, into this broken world,
    To be bearers of your hope,
            messengers of your judgment,
            ministers of your healing,
            proclaimers of your peace,
servants of your Son.

For it is in his name, the One whom we call the way and the life, that we pray. Amen.

Elizabeth C. Nordbeck is the Moses Brown Professor of Ecclesiastical History at Andover Newton Theological School, Newton Centre, Massachusetts.

O GOD, TENDER AND JUST

Study Guide

ABOUT THIS STUDY GUIDE

❀

THIS STUDY GUIDE EXPLORES the personal, congregational, and theological dimensions of not only the terrorist attacks of September 11, 2001, but also other unexpected, devastating events and circumstances. There are many important differences between reflecting on September 11 and reflecting on other events that disrupt our lives and disorient us. Specific historical, cultural, political, economic, ethical, and theological dimensions pertain to September 11. However, the events of September 11 raise questions common to tragic events, such as the nature and power of God, evil, and our human capacities. This guide allows for reflection on both.

Each session is designed for a forty-five- to sixty-minute small group discussion, but participants are encouraged to adapt the material to fit the needs of their particular group. The questions are intended to invite shared reflection and presume that participants have read the corresponding chapters in *O God, Tender and Just.*

The sessions begin with a song, include a prayer and questions for reflection, and conclude with another prayer. There is also a journaling question at the end of each session for individual use. Participants will need:

- Copies of this book, *O God, Tender and Just*

- Hymnals (Most selections in this study come from *The New Century Hymnal.* Section 4 recommends "God Be in My Head," which can be found in *The Pilgrim Hymnal.*)

- Bibles

It will be important for groups to create a safe space where participants can share openly without fear of being criticized or ostracized. Faithful people genuinely disagree on a variety of issues related to these themes. Deep issues take time and love to work through in community and cannot be "solved" in the confines of an hour. Listening for God's voice among the voices of our sisters and brothers is essential so that we may walk with one another and God through difficult times.

SECTION 1

❀

THE THINGS THAT WE FEAR COME UPON US: FIRST RESPONSES TO SEPTEMBER 11

GATHERING SONG

"What a Fellowship" (or "What a Covenant") (471) or
"A Mighty Fortress Is Our God" (439, 440) or
Nada Te Turbe (772)

PRAYER

God of mercy and strength, we open ourselves to your presence in this gathering. There is much to fear in our world, some of which we can name and some that we cannot. But we know that your perfect love casts out all fear. So with confidence and hope, we ask for you to be with us. In the name of Emmanuel, God with us, we pray. Amen.

OPENING (*5–10 minutes*)

When our worst fears become reality, there is no "correct" way to respond. Each of us needs and wants different things from one another and from God. Do you tend to seek company or solitude during difficult times? Why?

SHARED REFLECTION (*30–45 minutes*)

The Terrible Unexpected

- Which essay in this section best expresses what your first responses to September 11 were? How?

- Which feels the most remote to your experience? Why?

- What questions do you have for, or about, God in times of fear or tragedy?

On Evil

- Many people used the word "evil" to describe the events of September 11. Is this a word you would use? Why or why not? How can naming evil be helpful or not helpful? What are the dangers of naming someone or something evil?

- The United Church of Christ Statement of Faith includes the belief that God calls us into the church "to proclaim the gospel to all the world and resist the powers of evil." How does the church help us to resist the powers of evil?

On Salvation

- Unexpected tragedies cause us to reexamine what we believe about God and God's action in the world. We wonder about God's power and search for God's presence.

- What does it mean to say that God is our savior when horrible things happen? To what idols do we mistakenly turn for salvation?

- Where and how do you see God's saving action in the essays of this chapter?

UNISON PRAYER (Reinhold Niebuhr, 1943)

God, give us grace to accept with serenity the things that cannot be changed,
Courage to change the things that should be changed,
And the wisdom to distinguish the one from the other. Amen.

JOURNALING QUESTION

"Even though I walk through the darkest valley, I fear no evil; for you are with me" (Psalm 23:4a). How have you sensed God with you when you've walked through the darkest valley?

SECTION 2

❀

WE WHO ARE MANY ARE ONE BODY: THE PEOPLE OF GOD COME TOGETHER

GATHERING SONG

"Blessed Be the Tie That Binds" (393) or
"In Christ There Is No East or West" (394, 399)

PRAYER

Loving God, we know that Jesus prayed that we may all be one. Especially during difficult and uncertain times, we are thankful for our sisters and brothers who make Christ's love real to us. As we reflect on what it means to be a part of the body of Christ, we ask you to draw us into communion with your people everywhere, bearing each other's burdens, and encouraging each other in the faith. Amen.

OPENING *(5–10 minutes)*

This section contains letters from Christian communities around the world that are addressed to us as brothers and sisters in Christ. How do the letters illustrate what it means to be the body of Christ in the world?

SHARED REFLECTION *(30–45 minutes)*

A Suffering Body

- What counsel do you hear from the letters that express empathy for our suffering because of the terrible suffering the people in Colombia, Palestine, and El Salvador have experienced?

- Writing from Turkey, a predominantly Muslim country, Alison Stendahl gives us a glimpse of how the Turkish press and Muslim people condemned the attacks of September 11. What impact does the letter have on you? Would it feel the same if it came from Australia? Why or why not?

A Global Body

- What insight or perspective does being a part of the world-wide body of Christ provide for understanding and responding to September 11 as Christians in the United States? What is reinforced? What is called into question?

- What is your sense of how our brothers and sisters in Christ around the world perceive the United States?

- What do these letters ask us as a church to do in this nation?

- What might happen if all churches around the world participated vigorously in the Decade to Overcome Violence now being celebrated by the World Council of Churches?

A Sacramental Body

- Riad Jarjour, general secretary of the Middle East Council of Churches writes, "We break one bread and are one Body. Holding to that reality with a firm grip, you will rise above this tragic moment and, with you, we too will rise." Has the sacrament of Holy Communion provided strength and created community during terrible times? What does it mean to you that Christians around the world hold this celebration in common?

- What connections do you see between sharing in Holy Communion and living with justice and peace as the church universal? Which images and metaphors in the sacrament help you make sense of both tragedy and hope?

- Wilhelm Hueffmeier, president of the Evangelical Church of the Union in Germany refers to the presence of German firefighters at a memorial service in Potsdam as a "living experience" of Full Communion or *Kirchengemeinschaft*. How have you experienced "full communion" in these letters from our sisters and brothers in Christ around the world?

UNISON PRAYER (World Peace Prayer)

Lead us from death to life, from falsehood to truth, from despair to hope, from fear to trust. Lead us from hate to love, from war to peace; let peace fill our hearts, let peace fill our world, let peace fill our universe. Amen.

JOURNALING QUESTION

Dr. Bas Plaisier, from the United Protestant Churches in the Netherlands, writes, "Deep-rooted violence is manifest in many conflicts in our world. Together we are part of the underlying tensions." How has Christianity knowingly or unknowingly contributed to violence in our world? How does Christianity help us resist violence in our world?

SECTION 3

❀

WHAT ARE WE TO SAY ABOUT THESE THINGS?
THEOLOGICAL REFLECTIONS ON SEPTEMBER 11

GATHERING SONG

"When Sudden Terror Tears Apart" ("A New Hymn," Carl Daw, Section Three in *O God, Tender and Just*.) Suggested tunes: Bangor, Detroit, CMD, Third Mode Melody or
"O God Our Help in Ages Past" (25) or
"Immortal, Invisible, God Only Wise" or
"Over My Head" (514)

PRAYER

God of many names, we confess that though we know you only in part, we often presume to understand all of your ways. Grant us imagination, humility, and courage as we give voice to our questions and hopes. We pray in the name of the one whose love will not let us go, Jesus Christ. Amen.

OPENING (*5–10 minutes*)

What was your experience of God in and around the events of September 11? Have you known God's presence in the midst of other "sudden terrors?"

SHARED REFLECTION (*30–45 minutes*)
On Justice: God's and Ours

- Gabriel Fackre insists that a Just Peace Church must be concerned with bringing wrongdoers to justice as a part of its creed "to resist evil." Of what should Christians be mindful when seeking justice through human processes and institutions? How is God's justice made visible or obscured in human justice?

God's Reign

- What is the meaning of God's reign in the midst of terrible things? How does God reign?
- What are our obligations to God's realm?

God's Character

- Has your understanding of God been challenged or changed by the events of September 11?

- What names or characteristics of God surface for you when reflecting on these events (e.g. Refuge and Strength, Judge, Shepherd, Advocate, Protector, Liberator, Avenger, Rock, Mother Hen)?

Easter Seriousness

- In what ways do we (or did we before September 11, 2001) consider ourselves self-sufficient?

- How does the reality of Easter challenge our claims to self-sufficiency?

- What does resurrection look like in our "contested" world where God's good will struggles against the "deathliness of evil?"

The Church's Analysis Is Essential

- Many church leaders played prominent roles in public memorial services that provided comfort and assurance following September 11. Walter Brueggemann contends that the church has more than comfort to offer: It has a prophetic, biblical analysis that can help us get to the heart of questions of power and violence in our world. What counsel does the prophetic biblical tradition have for us? What are some of the ways the church can offer such analysis to its members and to the nation? How might we act on that prophetic message around the world?

- Jerry Falwell and Pat Robertson offered an analysis that blamed the events of September 11 on "abortionists, gays, and feminists." Many charged them with leveraging this terrible event for their own agendas. Many felt that these statements created further hurt and division within the Christian community and charged them with leveraging this terrible event for their own agenda. How does the church interpret tragic events in the public square with integrity?

Hope

- Otis Young reminds us that, in the midst of seemingly hopeless conditions in the nation, and while in jail himself, the prophet Jeremiah bought a field "as a sign of his confidence that this people, this world, had a future under God." What concrete actions have you or your community of faith taken as a sign of hope in difficult times, either at home or internationally?

God's Will

- In her book *Prayer and Our Bodies*, Flora Slosson Wuellner, drawing upon the work of Ron DelBene, explains that sometimes we think of God's will as a ten-ton elephant that's about to drop on our heads. In Hebrew and Greek, the word we translate as "will" more accurately means "yearning," as between two people in love. What is your understanding of God's will in tragic situations?

Prayer

- M. Douglas Meeks invites us to pray "in the company of Jesus" who, because of his own experience of terror and violence "can stand with all who suffer from any kind of terrorism." What does praying in the company of Jesus guard against? What does it invite, allow, or exclude from our prayers?

PRAYERFUL AFFIRMATION OF FAITH

A New Creed (United Church of Canada, 1980)

We are not alone; we live in God's world. We believe in God, who has created and is creating; who has come in Jesus, the Word made flesh, to reconcile and make new, who works in us and others by the Spirit. We trust in God. We are called to be the Church: to celebrate God's presence, to love and serve others, to seek justice and resist evil, to proclaim Jesus, crucified and risen, our judge and our hope. In life, in death, in life beyond death, God is with us. We are not alone. Thanks be to God. Amen.

JOURNALING QUESTION

Consider Rosemary McCombs Maxey's questions: How may I join with others of my faith to denounce the terrors of evil, and how may I bring myself to participate in acts of justice so that healing and peace may become real?

SECTION 4

❁

EVERY GOOD PATH: SUPPORTING FAITH WITH KNOWLEDGE

GATHERING SONG

"We Limit Not the Truth of God" (316) or
"Praise the Source of Faith and Learning" (411) or
"God Be in My Head" (*The Pilgrim Hymnal*)

PRAYER

God, our faith compels us to seek knowledge and try to understand your world. With humility, we lay aside all that would shield us from truth. (*Silence*). Guide us, so that with intelligence and compassion we may bear witness to your gospel of love in painful and uncertain times. Amen.

OPENING (*5–10 minutes*)

What are your sources for news and information about the world? How do you assess their reliability?

SHARED REFLECTION (*30–45 minutes*)

An Interconnected World

- In your daily life, do you typically feel connected to or isolated from the global community? Explain.

- Rabbi Michael Lerner suggests that we must recognize and respond to the sacred in each other as an antidote to using others. What do you think this means in concrete terms for us as Christians and as a nation?

A World of Many Faiths

- How do you interpret and assess non-Christian faiths?

- How do we build momentum for what Max Stackhouse describes as a "new kind of non-imperial, culturally pluralistic world-wide responsibility" that has as its goal a "Godly just peace?"

Avoiding Distortion

- Sometimes in our efforts to understand and interpret crises, we fail to take into account the complexity of the persons and histories involved. We assume; we predict; we sometimes stereotype. How have you seen these tendencies at work in the public square as well as in private conversation related to the events of September 11? How do you respond?

Human Rights

- Consider the list of rights and freedoms that Abraham Magendzo Kolstrein names as endangered. Do you share his concerns? Why or why not? Do you have additional concerns?

- Under what circumstances, if any, do you believe the rights of others should be suspended? Whose rights should be suspended? How should the decision to suspend rights be made? When and how should rights be restored?

- The Universal Declaration of Human Rights (found at <www.un.org>) sets minimal standards for ensuring that all people live in dignity and freedom. Do you think it captures all that is necessary for God's vision of justice and peace in our world?

Cultural Difference and Blending

- Barbara Brown Zikmund writes, "I find myself thinking that beyond language and culture, decent people all over the world have been profoundly affected by what happened on September 11. Suddenly we are all neighbors in a new way." To many Christians around the world, it seems that the United States was brought into the community of living with terror only recently. In what ways have you experienced language and culture being transcended by a common human connection?

PRAYER (Traditional Prayer from Kenya)

From the cowardice that dares not face new truth,
From the laziness that is contented with half-truth,
From the arrogance that thinks it knows all truth,
Good Lord, deliver me. Amen.

JOURNALING QUESTION

How has your faith changed or grown by what you've learned over this past year about our world?

SECTION 5

❀

FAITH WORKS: RESPONDING TO DISASTER WITH ACTION

GATHERING SONG

"God of Grace and God of Glory" (436) or
"God, Speak to Me That I May Speak"(531) or
"*Cuando El Pobre*" ("When a Poor One") or
"*Thuma Mina*" ("Send Me Lord") (360)

PRAYER

God, who acts to save in every generation, we come before you to reflect on our actions and our inactions. In your mercy, transform the compulsion that drives us to "do" and the apathy that lulls us into doing nothing. We seek a deeper understanding of what it means to make our faith visible in your wounded and suffering world. Amen.

OPENING (*5–10 minutes*)

Is it easier for you to give help or to receive help? Why?

SHARED REFLECTION (*30–45 minutes*)

- In what ways have you seen the church respond in times of disaster? What strengths and resources do faith communities, in particular, have to offer? What makes it difficult for us or for our church or nation to act in times of crisis and uncertainty?

- How do we examine the effectiveness of our responses to crisis? How can we examine our responses to chronic problems? For example, following the September 11 attacks, many people donated blood, not all of which was necessary because the deceased so greatly outnumbered the injured. Was this a symbolic action? Is there a role for symbolic actions in responding to crises?

- How do actions of solidarity (for example, wearing a *hijab*) differ from actions of assistance (for example, providing financial help)? How are each important and how might they impact or interpret each other?

- Some of what we "do" in the midst of crises involves speaking out about difficult or controversial things. How does our speaking make possible new ways of "doing?" How does our listening change our actions?

- How is worship faithful action?

- In the United States, we have the opportunity to affect public policy through advocacy. What does the church's voice bring to debates on public policy?

CLOSING PRAYER (Alan Paton, South Africa)

O Lord, open my eyes that I may see the needs of others; open my ears that I may hear their cries; open my heart so that they need not be without succor; let me not be afraid to defend the weak because of the anger of the strong, nor afraid to defend the poor because of the anger of the rich. Show me where love and hope and faith are needed, and use me to bring them to those places. And so open my eyes and my ears that I may this coming day be able to do some work of peace for thee. Amen.*

JOURNALING QUESTION

Do your actions mirror your words? Is your listening as deep as your speaking? Where do you need to bring your words and actions into alignment? What things do you need to intentionally say? What things do you need to concretely do?

*Alan Paton, "Instrument of Thy Peace," *The United Methodist Hymnal: Book of United Methodist Worship* (Nashville, Tenn.: United Methodist Publishing House, 1989). Copyright ©1968, 1982 Seabury Press, c/o Harper & Row Publishers, Inc.; 10 E 53rd St; New York, New York 10022.

SECTION 6

❈

TO LIVE PEACEABLY WITH ALL: REFLECTIONS ON WAR AND PEACE

GATHERING SONG

"God of the Ages, Who with Sure Command" (592) or
"For the Healing of the Nations"(576) or
"O for a World" (575)

PRAYER

We gather with humility and openness to seek your word to us, O God. Show us how to live peaceably with all. Make us sensible and imaginative that we may not create violence or oppression and may be ambassadors of reconciliation. In the name of Jesus Christ who births the new creation. Amen.

OPENING QUESTION (5–10 *minutes*)

For what are you willing to sacrifice or give your life? For what are you willing to live your life?

SHARED REFLECTION (30–45 *minutes*)

- A Just Peace is "the interrelation of friendship, justice, and common security from violence." Those who work for a just peace encourage the active promotion of peace and justice during times of peace as well as war. How can peace and justice be actively promoted during times of war? During times of peace? You may wish to consult the "Pronouncement on Affirming the United Church of Christ as a Just Peace Church" (found at <www.ucc.org/justice>).

- The phrase "just peace" is often used to translate the biblical word, *shalom.* Shalom means well-being for all, not only those who have the money or the strength to secure it for themselves. It is a profoundly interdependent vision of creation. When the prophet Jeremiah counsels Jews in exile to seek the well-being of Babylon and Jesus exhorts us to love our enemies, we are challenged to see those who oppose us as also part of God's intention for our common good. How do we, as Christians, work against violence and oppression and for God's vision of shalom while not "becoming the evil we deplore?"

- Reflect on the following statement by Martin Luther King Jr.: "Violence may murder the murderer, but it doesn't murder murder. Violence may murder the liar, but it doesn't murder lie; it doesn't establish truth. Violence may even murder the dishonest man, but it doesn't murder dishonesty. Violence may go to the point of murdering the hater, but it doesn't murder hate. It may increase hate. It is always a descending spiral leading nowhere. This is the ultimate weakness of violence: It multiplies evil and violence in the universe. It doesn't solve any problems."*

- Do you agree with Scott Simon's implication that the war against terrorism today is similar to the war against fascism? Are Christians called to preserve democracy?

- What are the implications for Christians of Jesus' teaching, "repay no one evil for evil"? How do you think Jesus would respond to terrorism?

- How has your Christian faith shaped your support of or dissent from war?

PRAYER

O God who suffers with us, we cry out to you on behalf of our world—divided by war, ravaged by violence, oppressed by poverty, and silenced by oppression. We especially remember this day . . . *(petitions may be offered silently or aloud)*. God, in your mercy, heal and bless your people. Grant us the joy of living into your vision where all creation is whole and well. Animate our hearts, our words, and our actions, that we may be bearers of hope. Guide us so that we may make visible your realm of justice and peace in our world. We pray in the name of Jesus Christ, Prince of Peace. Amen.

JOURNALING QUESTION

What connections do you see between personal healing and social transformation? How do you nurture shalom within yourself? How do you connect that to your external practice of shalom?

*Martin Luther King Jr., speech at staff retreat, 14 November 1966 in Kansas City. Qtd. in James H. Cone, *Martin and Malcolm and America: A Dream or a Nightmare* (Maryknoll, N.Y.: Orbis Books, 1991), 270.